# Reformed Theology for the Third Christian Millennium
The Sprunt Lectures 2001

*Edited by B. A. Gerrish*

Westminster John Knox Press
LOUISVILLE • LONDON

© 2003 Westminster John Knox Press

Scripture quotations, unless otherwise indicated, are from the New Revised Standard Version of the Bible, copyright © 1989 by the Division of Christian Education of the National Council of the Churches of Christ in the U.S.A., and used by permission.

Scripture quotations marked RSV are taken from the Revised Standard Version of the Bible, copyright © 1946, 1952, 1971, and 1973 by the Division of Christian Education of the National Council of the Churches of Christ in the U.S.A., and are used by permission.

*Book design by Sharon Adams*
*Cover design by Lisa Buckley*

*First edition*
Published by Westminster John Knox Press
Louisville, Kentucky

This book is printed on acid-free paper that meets the American National Standards Institute Z39.48 standard. ♾

PRINTED IN THE UNITED STATES OF AMERICA

03 04 05 06 07 08 09 10 11 12 — 10 9 8 7 6 5 4 3 2 1

Library of Congress Cataloging-in-Publication Data is on file at the Library of Congress, Washington, D.C.

0-664-22586-1

# Contents

Preface                                                                    vii

Introduction: Doing Theology in the Reformed Tradition
    *B. A. Gerrish*                                      1

1. Holy Beauty: A Reformed Perspective on Aesthetics within a
   World of Ugly Injustice
       *John W. de Gruchy*                               13
2. The Theology and Ethics of Martin Luther King Jr.:
   Contributions to Christian Thought and Practice
       *Peter J. Paris*                                   27
3. Reformed Theology and Modern Culture
       *Jan Rohls*                                        45
4. The Living God: The Problem of Divine Personality in
   Reformed Theology
       *Dawn DeVries*                                     61
5. Justice and Justification
       *Nicholas Wolterstorff*                           83

Contributors                                                               97
Notes                                                                      99
Index of Scriptural Citations                                             109
Index of Persons                                                          111
Index of Subjects                                                         115

# Preface

The chapters of this book began as the Sprunt Lectures delivered at Union Theological Seminary and Presbyterian School of Christian Education (Union-PSCE), Richmond, Virginia, on January 24–26, 2001. They are published here in the order in which they were originally presented. The annual Sprunt lectureship was established in 1911 by James Sprunt, a ruling elder in the Presbyterian Church of Wilmington, North Carolina. Over the years, it has brought to the campus of Union-PSCE some of the most eminent scholars and theologians in the academy and the churches.

The 2001 series of lectures departed from the usual pattern in two respects. First, instead of a single lecturer, five theologians were invited to share their thoughts on the prospects for Reformed theology in the third Christian millennium, and the series concluded with a lively panel discussion among them. Second, the lectures were cosponsored by the Institute for Reformed Theology (IRT), established at Union-PSCE in 1998 with a grant from the Lilly Endowment.

The idea of the Institute arose from the conviction that the Reformed tradition has a wealth of theological resources to contribute to ecumenical theology in our day. At the same time, we were convinced of an urgent need for informed and mutually respectful conversations among pastors and professional theologians of diverse theological persuasions. Hence, the central feature of the Institute's program has been a series of year-long colloquies, in which a good mixture of theologians, pastors, and students from across the nation were invited to study and discuss together some aspect of contemporary Christian life and thought in the light of the resources, but also the deficiencies, of the Reformed tradition. Thus far, there have been colloquies on sin and repentance, divine activity, public ethics, grace, and the Word of God. By all accounts, the colloquies have evoked an extraordinarily enthusiastic response. The opportunities—all too rare—for conversation between pastors and professors have sparked an interest in closing a communication gap in the life of the churches, and it is hoped that the seed money awarded for a four-year period by the Lilly Endowment will generate funding for a permanent Institute of Reformed Theology.

As an adjunct to the colloquies, there have been series of IRT lectures by distinguished church leaders from North America and beyond, and it was natural enough that at some point the Institute and the Sprunt lectureship should combine resources, since their goals have partly coincided. The 2001 Sprunt Lectures, cosponsored by the IRT, were the result. Since I was present at the time of the lectures as both a visiting professor of theology at Union-PSCE and a cofounder of the Institute, I was happy to accept the invitation to edit the lectures for publication and to contribute a brief introductory reflection on what it may mean to do theology in a confessional tradition. I am grateful for the prompt and cordial cooperation I received from the lecturers. They are identified in the list of contributors by their current positions and two or three of their publications most likely to be of interest to readers of this book.

B. A. Gerrish

# Introduction: Doing Theology in the Reformed Tradition

*B. A. Gerrish*

> *The safety of that man hangs by a thread whose defense turns wholly on this—that he has constantly adhered to the religion handed down to him from his forefathers.*
>
> —Calvin, *Reply to Sadoleto*

> *Our constant endeavor, day and night, is to form in the manner we think will be best whatever is faithfully handed on by us.*
>
> —Calvin, *Defense against Pighius*

Why *Reformed* theology in the third Christian millennium? The heyday of self-consciously "confessional" theologies is long past. They developed in the sixteenth century, in the wake of the Protestant Reformation and its failure to achieve the goal of a single reformed church in Western Christendom. On the continent of Europe, the result was the reluctant coexistence of three main churches, each claiming exclusive possession of sound doctrine. Of course there was always agreement, too—more than polemical ardor allowed the adversaries, usually, to admit. But Roman Catholicism, Lutheranism, and Calvinism each defined themselves in creeds or confessions framed in conscious opposition to the beliefs of the other two. In this sense, their theologies were all "confessional." In the canons and decrees of the Council of Trent (1545–63), the Roman Church drew the line against the presumed heresies of the day; the Lutherans did the same, with a different set of heresies, in their *Book of Concord* (1580), and so did the Calvinists in a series of family-related "Reformed" confessions. Throughout the seventeenth century, duty required a faithful church member to suppose, though with decreasing plausibility, that

1

his or her own church had a monopoly on pure doctrine. But the slide into pluralism had begun.

## CONFESSIONAL THEOLOGY IN A PLURALISTIC DAY

The number of rival churches did not stop at three. The so-called Anabaptists, harassed by Roman Catholics, Lutherans, and Calvinists alike, were there from the start. In time, the proliferation of religious groups in Britain and still more in America, where the severance of ties between church and state encouraged division and novelty, led to the extreme pluralistic situation in which we now stand. Peter Berger characterizes it as a "market situation," in which each of us is free to choose from an astonishing variety of religious options. Although a measure of "product loyalty" may persist, as Berger says, the market militates against religious traditionalism.[1] It must be added that *theological* pluralism goes beyond *denominational* divisions. At least since the eighteenth century, the emergence of new intellectual and spiritual movements has created party loyalties alongside denominational loyalties. A Reformed pietist and a Reformed rationalist in eighteenth-century Germany, for instance, would have found less in common with each other than each would have found with his or her Lutheran counterpart. Throughout the succeeding two centuries religious alliances, such as the coalition of "evangelicals," have assumed greater importance in defining theological standpoint than does denominational membership.

Not surprisingly, the walls between the divided churches have been crumbling. The preservation of a confessional tradition in American Protestantism seems to work only where a strong ethnic tie persists, and ethnic ties are themselves eroding. Believers move freely from church to church for many reasons, not because of denominational affiliation alone—or even mainly. Old boundaries have become permeable, and the question must be honestly faced whether it makes sense anymore to insist on confessional differences that once justified a separate existence. It may even be that in the third Christian millennium our theological horizon will, and should, increasingly extend beyond the ecumenical problem of pluralism within Christianity to the global problem of Christianity's place among the world's religions. And where does that leave Reformed theology?

It would be a mistake to infer from the "market situation" that recognition of de facto pluralism and of the ever-widening context of serious theological inquiry automatically entails the surrender of particularity, or even of an inflexible exclusivism. The question is whether particularity can be affirmed *without* exclusivism. There is no shortage of religious groups in America, both large and small, that persist in the belief that they have an exclusive claim to the possession of divine truth. The urge to separate, or to remain separated, from those thought to lack some portion of the fullness of truth remains strong even in the midst of earnest ecumenical and interfaith dialogue. Granted, it is not perhaps *impossible* that there may somewhere be unalloyed, unchanging truth without any mixture of error or with much less error than everywhere else. But even those who, like myself, think it *unlikely* do not need to deny the worth of a particular theological tradition. Rather, they will welcome the traditions as differing perspectives on a common reality, dependent on one another for the fullness of a truth that none of them possesses alone.

Further, they need not equate preservation of a theological tradition with drawing the wagons around the institution that fostered it. It is undeniable that many have been led to Christian faith through the particular vision of an individual religious community and find their loyalty to Christ nurtured by a continuing commitment to the community that first brought them to faith. But the faith is larger than the community that conveyed it. Particularity is not the same as exclusivism. And it is not relativism either—if relativism means abandonment of the effort to get closer to shared truth. The churches will approximate truth the more they listen for it together.

If this much is conceded, I see no obligation to rule out theology in the Reformed tradition or in any other tradition either. Surprisingly, as it happens, the closing years of the twentieth century witnessed a remarkable new interest in Reformed identity. Conferences on the prospects for Reformed theology were held in Germany, Britain, and the United States, and research centers for the study of Reformed history and theology were established in Amsterdam, Cambridge, and Richmond, Virginia. A substantial volume has emerged;[2] others are on the way.[3] But what *is* theology in the Reformed tradition? What *is* Reformed theology?

## THEOLOGY IN THE REFORMED TRADITION

It might be thought sufficient to answer that Reformed theology is theology produced by theologians who belong to one or another of the Reformed churches. But, on reflection, that obviously won't do. It invites the prior question, *which* churches are Reformed? Some of the older literature on comparative church studies—"comparative symbolics," as it used to be called—was inclined to classify as "Reformed" anyone left over after Eastern Orthodoxy, Roman Catholicism, and Lutheranism had been presented—including Anglicans, Baptists, and (sometimes) Methodists.[4] We might shorten the list by confining it to the membership of the World Alliance of Reformed Churches (WARC), which includes Presbyterians and Congregationalists along with many, but not all, churches that have "Reformed" in their titles. The Constitution of the Alliance (emended in 1982) expects of its member churches a "position in faith and evangelism" that is "in general agreement with that of the historic Reformed confessions." Could this be taken to indicate the character of Reformed theology as a particular kind of confessional theology?

Obviously, the intent of the constitution is to allow a measure of latitude. The

Reformed churches have usually differed from Lutheranism in the mitigated stringency with which they require adherence to their historic statements of faith. They lack a closed book of confessions. The number of old confessions is large, and new ones are continually being made.[5] We speak hopefully of a family resemblance among the old and the new, but the resemblance isn't obvious anymore, and no creed or collection of creeds was ever designed to have permanent authority over all the Reformed churches. Each confession was understood to belong to a particular time and place, and the recognition of particularity carried with it an admission of reformability.

Greater uniformity has sometimes been secured by assigning to one confession a unique—though local—authority. This is what the Presbyterians did with their Westminster Confession (1647). But the long struggle over the "subscription" required of ministers in the Presbyterian churches unquestionably weakened the confession's authority. The formula under which my generation of Presbyterian candidates for the ministry were ordained in the Presbyterian Church in the U.S.A. was considered moderate: "Do you sincerely receive and adopt the [Westminster] Confession of Faith and the Catechism of this Church, as containing the system of doctrine taught in the Holy Scriptures?" Some of us thought that could be better said. (*Is* it a "system of doctrine" that the Scriptures teach?) The Presbyterian Church (U.S.A.) now has a whole *Book of Confessions,* and the ordination formula asks more flexibly: "Will you be instructed and led by those confessions as you lead the people of God?" and "Will you be a minister of the Word and Sacrament in obedience to Jesus Christ, under the authority of Scripture, and continually guided by our confessions?" That, I think, is an improvement, and it does not exclude the right and duty of the church's theologians to be critical of the confessions, where necessary. In practice, however, it offers very little help on the question how, exactly, or how regularly, a theologian will use the historic and contemporary standards of the church. You should not expect to identify a Presbyterian theologian by the number of his or her citations from the confessions, though a total absence of such citations might raise a legitimate doubt.

A more reliable clue is to be found in the *theologians* cited. The Reformed churches have been blessed with a succession of great theologians. They find it hard to speak of them without the sin of pride. John Calvin, Jonathan Edwards, Friedrich Schleiermacher, Karl Barth, among others, were all theological pacesetters in their generation and continue to provide insight and inspiration in ours. But one name in this abbreviated list betrays the fact that here, too, lies a problem if we are looking for ways to define theology in the Reformed tradition. For decades, Schleiermacher has served as the favorite whipping boy of the church he loved and served so faithfully, and it is widely supposed that he betrayed the Reformed tradition. This is not the place to argue for what I believe is his immense importance to the progress of Reformed theology. The point, for now, is that a tradition is evidently not simply discovered and traced through history; rather, it is always in some measure a construct on the part of those who look back from the present and believe they may exclude from the lineage a major thinker once regarded as the renewer of Reformed theology. Behind their belief may lie a static view of tradition.

There will always be a sharp difference between those who understand faithfulness to tradition as the *preservation* of past doctrines and those who understand it as the recognition that past doctrines may be worthy of *development*. Charles Hodge, for example, took the language of tradition, like the language of sacred Scripture, to be immobile. Hence, when reading Calvin, he could either agree with what he read or (occasionally) disagree: there was no third option. Schleiermacher, by contrast, wrestled with Calvin's ideas—notably, his doctrine of election—and tried to formulate them anew. Interestingly, that was how Calvin received the Reformation principles he inherited from Luther. When accused by a Roman Catholic adversary, Albert Pighius, of diverging from Luther's opinions on free will, Calvin replied: "If Pighius does not know it, I want to make this plain to him: our constant endeavor, day and night, is to *form* in the manner we think will be best whatever is faithfully *handed on* by us."[6] *Fideliter tradere* is always *formare*. There is an affinity between Schleiermacher's use of Calvin and Calvin's use of Luther. We might even venture to say that here is the distinctively Reformed understanding of tradition: theology, like the Reformed church itself, is *reformata et semper reformanda*.

May we then conclude that Reformed theology is not simply indoctrination by means of past and present confessions but persistent wrestling with the best thinking we can find among our forebears, not excluding the thoughts they embodied in the church's statements of faith? I believe so, and I have attempted to argue the point by making a distinction between dogmas and habits of mind as the heart of doing theology in the Reformed tradition.[7]

## ESSENTIAL TENETS OR GOOD HABITS?

The plea is often heard that, although not every letter of the Reformed confessions can be binding on the church's leaders, the highest court of the church should decide what are the "essential tenets" that Reformed theologians are expected to uphold, or at least not to contradict. The essential tenets are sometimes identified with the so-called Reformed distinctives, but that could be misleading. What is most essential to Reformed faith is not what is peculiar to it but what it shares with other catholic and evangelical communions. This is not to say that the particular is trivial and disposable. We have already seen reason not to eliminate the particular, which may very well *mediate* the essential, though it is not identical with it, and we could certainly say that the Reformed faith would not be what it is without its particularities. But as the preface to the Brief Statement of Faith of the Presbyterian Church (U.S.A.) puts it: "The faith we confess unites us with the one, universal church. The most important beliefs of Presbyterians are those we share with other Christians, and especially with other evangelical Christians who look to the Protestant Reformation as a renewal of the gospel of Jesus Christ."[8]

Various attempts have been made over the years to state the essential tenets. If we look back to Calvin himself, we find a churchman appalled by the scandal of divisions in the church and an astute diagnostician of the human vanity that often motivates them. He warned against separation for frivolous or insufficient reasons, whether of faith or of life. And yet Calvin insisted that "some [articles of doctrine] are so necessary to know that they should be certain and unquestioned by all . . . as the proper principles of religion."[9] He did not continue, however, with an exhaustive list of them. He simply added: "Such are: God is one; Christ is God and the Son of God; our salvation rests in God's mercy; and the like." The list is short, and not one of the items on it asserts a "Reformed distinctive."

Very different are the familiar lists that came into being later, usually in response to theological controversies. They are more specific, and some are self-consciously Reformed. There are the so-called Five Points of Calvinism, for example, derived from the condemnation of Arminianism by the Reformed Synod of Dort (1618–19): total depravity, unconditional election, limited atonement, irresistible grace, and the perseverance of the saints (TULIP). Or there's the list of five essential doctrines drawn up by the General Assembly of the American Presbyterians in 1910, when the fundamentalist controversy was gaining momentum: the inerrancy of the Bible, the virgin birth, substitutionary atonement, Christ's bodily resurrection, and his miracles. The alliance of old-school Presbyterians with the dispensationalists added to the list of "fundamentals" the eschatological doctrines of heaven and hell and the second coming of Christ. Or, again, there is the list given in the present *Constitution* of the Presbyterian Church (U.S.A.) to describe the faith of the Reformed tradition: one central theme, the sovereignty of God, and four related themes—election for salvation and service, a covenant life of disciplined concern for order, stewardship in the use of God's gifts, and the call to work for justice.[10]

The difficulty with these checklists is that they change. Like the confessions of the Reformed churches, they are occasional documents written to meet the needs of a particular time and place. They do not define the essential tenets of the Reformed churches for *all* time; the church may later correct, modify, or gently abandon them—at least in part. The obvious example is the Presbyterian Declaratory Statement of 1903, which professes to interpret the doctrine of double predestination but actually dismantles it.[11] Of course, it does not necessarily follow that the attempt to define the Reformed tradition in a list of essential doctrines is fruitless. There may in fact be material continuity in doctrine, and it seems to me quite proper to try anew, in each generation, to state what it is. But the results will never be final, and it may be better to locate the continuity, first of all, not in the doctrinal conclusions of any one generation but in the manner in which the Reformed go about the task of *reaching* their conclusions: in short, not in perennial dogmas but in a certain habit of mind, which it is the goal of education in the church's seminaries to impart or nurture. I think the Reformed habit of mind exhibits at least five characteristics.

First, it is *deferential:* a habit of deference to our forebears. This follows from the very concept of tradition. We don't begin our theology *de novo.* We pass the torch on, and if we see far, it is because we stand on the shoulders of giants. To put it in plain terms, it is a question of which books we reach for first when we want to think as Reformed theologians: the Scriptures and the confessions first, to be sure, but then the works of the great succession of Reformed divines. And this requires us not simply to be abreast of the *newest* books, which may have only a short life expectancy, but to be at home in the *classics,* which have proved their enduring value and on which the latest theology is bound to be more or less dependent.

Second, however, the Reformed habit of mind is just as fundamentally *critical*—even of the "fathers." This must be so; otherwise, theology (properly so called) could not exist. Theology is not mindless repetition of the past for the sake of indoctrination, but critical reflection on past and present alike for the sake of a stronger and purer witness of the church in the future. *Critical* deference is certainly a difficult, mediating principle. There is always the temptation to veer to one or the other side: impatience with tradition, or passive absorption of it. Anti-traditionalism is no doubt the stronger temptation these days. But recall Calvin's admonition to Sadoleto: "The safety of that man hangs by a thread whose defence turns wholly on this—that he has constantly adhered to the religion handed down to him from his forefathers."[12]

Third, the Reformed habit of mind is *open*—open to wisdom and truth wherever they are to be found. From the first, the Reformed were debtors at once to the Lutherans and the Renaissance humanists, creating what Calvin called a "Christian philosophy"—faithful to the gospel and deeply committed to learning. In a famous phrase, Schleiermacher described the twofold engagement of Protestant theology with living Christian faith and completely free scientific inquiry as an "eternal covenant," and he wrote: "It is my firm conviction that the basis for such a covenant was already established in the Reformation."[13] Wherever the authentic Reformed habit of mind has prevailed, the covenant has been faithfully kept, and it has ensured that the development of Reformed theology will be determined not merely by what is being said *in* the churches but by what is said *to* the churches by the world of learning outside.

Fourth, the Reformed habit of mind is *practical.* Truth, the old divines used to say, is "in order to" goodness. Not *all* truth but certainly *theological* truth: the knowledge of God is for the sake of the worship of God and for personal and social change. The duty of a theologian, Calvin says, is to teach things "true, sure, and profitable."[14] Naturally, it would never have occurred to Calvin to make utility the criterion of truth. But he had no interest in what he dismissed as mere "speculation," and he believed it necessary to restrain mere "curiosity." Here is the impetus not only behind the characteristically Calvinist preoccupation with edification and sanctification but also behind the equally characteristic drive to transform society into a mirror of God's glory.

Fifth, and last, the Reformed habit of mind is *evangelical* in the precise sense in which the description was used at the time of the Reformation. It is the habit of continually bringing theological reflection back to the gospel. The preface to the Scots Confession declares: "We call on God to record that . . . with all humility we embrace the purity of Christ's Gospel, which is the one food of our souls and therefore so precious to us that we are determined to suffer the greatest of worldly dangers, rather than let our souls be defrauded of it."[15]

It would be gross presumption to speak as though Calvinists alone exhibited this habit of mind, and a manifest exaggeration to claim that every Reformed theologian exhibits all of its characteristics equally, all the time. The balance among the five shifts from time to time, from theologian to theologian, and from day to day in the work of a single theologian. But if we attempt to describe Reformed theology not in terms of any set of fixed doctrines but in terms of a collective activity that exhibits a characteristic (not unique) habit of mind, the description would go something like this: Reformed theology is an ongoing conversation into which the "fathers" of the Reformed church are drawn, deferentially but not uncritically; in which openness to sacred and secular learning brings continual new light, always with an eye to the practice of piety and the transformation of human lives, both individually and socially; and in which, finally, the focus returns again and again to the meaning of the gospel. Such a description would of course be fraudulent if it had no empirical grounding in what Reformed theologians are actually doing, as well as documentation from the history of Reformed theology. But I would be surprised if readers of the following chapters did not detect the distinctive Reformed habit of mind in the Sprunt Lectures for 2001.

## REFORMED THEOLOGY FOR THE
## THIRD CHRISTIAN MILLENNIUM

The series begins with a chapter that may evoke surprise. The Reformed vision of the world and God has undeniably inspired great literature, but the Reformed churches have frequently been judged insensitive or even hostile to the visual arts. Their reputation is not entirely deserved. True, among the Reformed the concern for truth and goodness has commonly outweighed appreciation for beauty, but John de Gruchy thinks it possible, as well as needful, to develop something like a Reformed aesthetic. It would by no means be detached from the passion for truth and justice. The prophetic protest against the seduction of an idolatrous aestheticism has its place. But de Gruchy, well known for his stand in the struggle against apartheid in South Africa, turns his attention in chapter 1 to the *ugliness* of apartheid and argues for the crucial role of art precisely in the social transformation that the continuing legacy of apartheid demands. Aesthetics in general, he says, is about the perception of reality through the imagination and the creative use of the imagination to change the way we see the world. Without beauty, truth and goodness lack the power to persuade. Hence art is not only, as Calvin believed, the gift of the Holy Spirit but also one of the means by which the Spirit works. Spiritual formation is not merely a matter of sound instruction: it may even be said to call for the cultivation of good taste, which shuns both philistinism and ecclesiastical kitsch. "Art in itself cannot change society, but good art, whatever its form, helps us both individually and corporately to perceive reality in a new way, and by so doing, it opens up possibilities of transformation."

In America as in South Africa, the elimination of racism has had to contend with a theological recalcitrance in which the Reformed have played their shameful part. The concern for justice in American Presbyterianism did not always entail a belief in the equality of all peoples. African Americans learned through suffering to recognize a common, inclusive humanity that transcends differences of race, and they learned it not for themselves alone but for an overwhelmingly white Presbyterian Church. In the telling words that Peter Paris quotes, by way of Gayraud S. Wilmore, from Leland Stanford Cozart, "Because of the Presbyterian Church, the Negro in America today is infinitely the richer in body, mind, and spirit; because of the Negro, the Presbyterian Church is immeasurably more responsive to human needs." In chapter 2, Paris recalls the unique ecumenical role Martin Luther King Jr. played during the 1960s in transforming the spiritual vision of so many Euro-Americans, including the Presbyterians, and sets out the theological and ethical principles that inspired King's prophetic vocation as minister of the gospel and social reformer. King believed in the sovereignty of God, the Liberator, Redeemer, and Friend of the oppressed; in the equality of all people under God; in the power of love and the policy of nonviolent resistance that it calls for; and in the eschatological vision of one "beloved community" of all humanity. He held to an unshakable faith that the universe was created as a moral order, in which justice must finally prevail.

While white Presbyterians and other Reformed Christians have hardly been at the forefront of the struggle against racism, many historians have held that Calvinism in general represents a more aggressive variety of Protestantism than Lutheranism and consequently has had a more powerful impact on Western culture. But there is certainly no consensus on the subject. Numerous historical studies argue, in detail, for a formative influence of Reformed theology on the economics, politics, art, and science of the Western world, and at least as many other studies find the supposed connections to be fanciful. The famous Stone Lectures delivered by the Dutch statesman-theologian Abraham Kuyper at Princeton Theological Seminary (1899) presented the classic case for Calvinism as a progressive force in the shaping of Western culture. A similarly comprehensive case was made in Germany by Ernst Troeltsch, who had been impressed by sociologist Max Weber's thesis about the link between the Protestant ethic and the spirit of modern capitalism. Jan Rohls reviews the arguments in chapter 3. He concludes that in actual fact Calvinist doctrine had no special significance for the progress of capitalism, democracy, painting, music, or natural science in

Continental Europe, and that in any case Kuyper, Weber, and Troeltsch all mis-represented Calvinism itself by their heavy emphasis on the doctrine of predesti-nation. The debate over the influence of Calvinism on the rise and progress of the modern world continues, especially in recent literature on the religious roots of democracy in America and of the scientific revolution in seventeenth-century England. For Rohls, however, the story is less about the impact of Calvinism on the surrounding culture, and more about the adaptation of Calvinists to their intellectual environment. The important question for the future is whether Reformed theologians will continue to regard reconciliation with modern cul-ture as a permanent task or will lapse into insularity and irrelevance.

No theme has been more consistently associated with Calvinism than "the sovereignty of God," often linked closely with the overexposed doctrine of dou-ble predestination. Calvin held that for the devout believer God's sovereignty is the ever-present care of a solicitous Father. But there are times when an earthly father is consumed with anguished love for his child while the heavenly Father seems strangely indifferent. Is the metaphor of a divine parent, after all, the best way of speaking about God? Is it right to think of God as a person? In chapter 4, Dawn DeVries reviews the thoughts of some of the most eminent Reformed theo-logians on these questions. The last century, she points out, saw an "intensifica-tion" of the concept of divine personality, whether grounded in God's self-revelation (Karl Barth, Emil Brunner), in moral experience (John Oman), or in the experience of Christian worship (H. H. Farmer). And yet, Oman and Farmer were careful to *qualify* the attribution of personality to God. Farmer, in particular, acknowledged the truth in criticisms aimed by Paul Tillich and others at the I-Thou model for encounter with God. In support of such caution and qualification, DeVries shows, Reformed theologians could well appeal to John Calvin, who taught that there is a hiddenness of God outside God's revelation and that even the language of revelation is accommodated to our slight capacity. And in the nineteenth century, Friedrich Schleiermacher and A. E. Biedermann, while affirming the religious need to picture God as a person, were forthright in their insistence on protecting Christian piety from the perils of unrestrained anthropomorphism. DeVries concludes that in the new millennium the problem of evil, the interface of science and religion, and an idolatrous piety must all send Reformed theology back, behind the intensification of personalistic descriptions of God in twentieth-century theology, to the reflections on the limits of person-alism in the older tradition.

The myth that Calvin made predestination the center of a systematic theol-ogy has long since been laid to rest, and the Reformed have always been less inclined than the Lutherans to make the gospel of justification by faith the chief article or center of evangelical doctrine. But Calvin did assign justification a spe-cial place as "the main hinge on which religion turns" and the "foundation . . . on which to build piety toward God."[16] In the Reformation controversy with Rome, only the interpretation of the Eucharist received as much attention as jus-tification by faith. And yet, historians are by no means of one mind in their explication of Luther's article of a standing or falling church; neither is there a full consensus among the biblical scholars on the meaning of the doctrine at its source, in Paul's letters to the Galatians and the Romans. The New Testament interpreters work largely from the antecedents of Paul's Greek vocabulary in the Hebrew Scriptures and from his more immediate background in Pharisaic Judaism and the Qumran literature. In chapter 5, Nicholas Wolterstorff takes a fresh look at justice and justification from the side of moral theory. The reluctance of the RSV translators to render Greek words of the *dik-* root by a common English equivalent (why not "just," "justice," and "justify" rather than "righteous," "righteousness," and "justify"?) may betray theological conditioning. It certainly reflects a perceived difference between "justice" and "righteousness," and this, Wolterstorff thinks, is correct. "Justice" is deeper in the moral order. Not to do what one ought to do is a failure of righteousness; a failure of justice is to *wrong* someone. "Righteousness is fully present when no one is guilty. Justice is fully present when no one is wronged." We are indeed unrighteous, but Paul's concern is that we have wronged God; hence God is angry. This is not to belittle *social* justice. But, as Calvin says, no one can injure his brother without wounding God. Justification is God's way of dealing not with our moral condition as such but with the fact that we have violated God's rights.

The five Sprunt lecturers for 2001 brought forth things both old and new out of their treasures and met in a lively conversation after the lectures ended. They chose very different themes for Reformed theology in the third Christian millennium, though each theme should prove predictably important, and they plainly differ from one another in how they go about their chosen tasks—even in the degree to which they value, appropriate, or correct the Reformed tradition. They do not represent a single theological standpoint, and no single thesis emerges—only the promise of a continuing conversation and good theology to come. This may disappoint readers who look for at least an agreed list of perennial Reformed "distinctives" with which to define (or circumscribe) the tradition. Others will be reassured to find that Reformed theology in the new millennium need not be rigid, parochial, complacent, or defensive.

# Chapter 1

# Holy Beauty: A Reformed Perspective on Aesthetics within a World of Ugly Injustice
*John W. de Gruchy*

Much of my theological endeavor over the years has focused on the struggle against apartheid in South Africa. During the past decade my focus has shifted to the relationship between Christianity and democratic transformation and, more recently, to theological aesthetics and to the role of art in transformation. This latter interest has clearly not meant a lessening of concern for theological engagement with public life. That remains constant out of both the conviction that theology and ethics cannot be separated and the fact that the struggle against the legacy of apartheid and injustice more generally remains. The transition to democracy requires an ongoing struggle for social transformation. My interest in theological aesthetics, then, is not an opting out of a commitment for social justice but an attempt to address a set of issues that have previously been neglected by those of us who were engaged as theologians in the struggle against apartheid. To emphasize this point, let me say that I wrote these words in the midst of a workshop on "Christianity, Art and Healing," where the focus was on the new holocaust facing sub-Saharan Africa: the HIV/AIDS pandemic. Nadine Gordimer, the celebrated South African novelist, has noted that art is "at the heart of liberation."[1] The struggle against apartheid certainly produced an artistic creativity of a remarkable kind and intensity.[2] It is remarkable, then, that theologians engaged in the struggle did not take this into account in doing theology.

## SOME PRELIMINARY ISSUES

Traditionally, beauty has been the key category for aesthetics. For much of the twentieth century, however, beauty was largely banished from aesthetics discourse. Aesthetics, it was rightly recognized, has a much broader focus. It has to do with the experience and perception of reality that we associate with the imagination and creativity, with metaphor and symbol, with games, playfulness, and friendship. The arts, whether fine or popular, in all their manifold forms, are central to aesthetics because they embody and express this dimension of experience; they evoke memories and suggest possibilities, thereby enabling us to see reality differently. As such aesthetics is about the arts, but it is about more than the arts. It is about perceiving reality in ways other than through rational enquiry and moral endeavor. It is about more than beauty—yet it is also about beauty. Indeed, as long as we recognize the broader contours of aesthetics, beauty remains the key category.

One reason why, for much of the twentieth century, beauty was banished from aesthetic discourse was in reaction to the aestheticism of those who pursued beauty for its own sake, a Romantic escapism oblivious to the ugly realities of a world gripped by oppression. In more recent times, precisely because of the ugliness of injustice, there has been a concerted attempt to recover beauty as the key category for aesthetic theory and praxis.[3] As Elaine Scarry has argued, the political complaints against beauty are incoherent; indeed, a commitment to beauty may well enhance our capacity to seek justice.[4] But, of course, *beauty*, like *justice*, is a contested term. "Whose beauty?" is as much a matter of contention as the question "Whose justice?" And the two are not unrelated.

One way to approach that question is through a consideration of its opposite, namely ugliness, and the way in which ugliness is represented in art. Not all art is what we would normally call beautiful. Much art protests the debasement of beauty in, for example, the advertising industry by producing works that are often shocking in their ugliness. It is often the case, Theodor Adorno observed, that "art has to make use of the ugly in order to denounce the world which creates and recreates ugliness in its own image."[5] But it is precisely this protest against unjust ugliness that reinforces the value and significance of beauty as something potentially redemptive. Indeed, if aesthetics were just about the beautiful, we would never really understand "the dynamic life inherent in the concept of beauty."[6]

My own exploration of aesthetics began through a growing awareness that apartheid was not only unjust but also ugly and that this was reflected in the architectural landscape of our country. In this regard we may recall

D.H. Lawrence's essay "Nottingham and the Mining Country" (1929), in which he wrote:

> The great crime which the moneyed classes and promoters of industry committed in the palmy Victorian days was the condemning of the workers to ugliness, ugliness, ugliness: meanness and formless and ugly surroundings, ugly ideals, ugly religion, ugly hope, ugly love, ugly furniture, ugly houses, ugly relationship between workers and employers. The human soul needs actual beauty even more than bread.[7]

If ugliness has the capacity to destroy life, so beauty, as Dostoyevsky so eloquently suggested, has the power to save the world.[8]

Like aesthetics more generally, theological aesthetics is about imagination and creativity. In pursuing this course of inquiry, theology enters into dialogue with the arts, just as it does with philosophy or the social sciences in its concern for truth and justice. But at its heart, theological aesthetics is about faith seeking to understand reality, not least the ugliness of injustice, from the perspective of the beauty of God revealed in creation and redemption. From this perspective, the reality of ugliness is subsumed within God's beauty, which, as Karl Barth insisted, "embraces death as well as life, fear as well as joy, what we might call the ugly as well as what we might call the beautiful."[9]

Theological aesthetics is thus grounded in our knowledge of God and of ourselves, as Calvin would have wanted, and as such it is not an optional extra for theology, something that might only attract the interest or satisfy the needs of aesthetically inclined Christians. Indeed, a failure to engage in theological aesthetics has dire consequences both for theology itself (that "beautiful science") and for the life and witness of the church. A concern for truth without goodness and beauty lacks the power to attract and convince those whose critical sensitivities are repelled by such dogmatism. A concern for goodness without truth or beauty—that is, without what Hans Urs von Balthasar called "graced form"—degenerates into barren moralism and misguided iconoclasm. In short, truth and goodness without beauty lack the power to convince and therefore to save.

Notwithstanding some notable exceptions, Jonathan Edwards being one of them, Reformed theology has been far more concerned historically about dogmatic truth and moral striving than it has been about aesthetic appreciation. Moreover, artistic creativity, especially through the visual and plastic arts, has often been regarded with reservation and suspicion rather than encouraged and celebrated as a source both of delight and of insight. This has not been universally so, and the Reformed tradition has too often been maligned by the uninformed. But there is enough truth in the criticism for us to take it seriously. The Reformed ethos has been chiefly one of truth and goodness rather than beauty, and of hearing and listening rather than of seeing and imagining. This being so, let me hasten to comment that theological aesthetics is not about giving priority to beauty over truth or goodness, nor does it imply the denigration of the word in favor of the image. Our concern is the Word of life whom we have "seen with our eyes . . . and touched with our hands" (1 John 1:1).

In this area as in any other, Reformed theology must be located within a broader ecumenical framework. Yet there is undoubtedly a Reformed theological perspective on aesthetics that needs to be considered within this framework, one shaped by our diverse yet coherent history of confession, worship, and witness. This has to do, first, with a commitment to the testimony of Scripture as witness to the triune God, creator and redeemer, confessed concretely within particular historical contexts. Such a witness, second, refuses to separate faith and public responsibility and is committed to the struggle for social transformation within particular historical contexts. Third, a Reformed approach to aesthetics recognizes the distinctions between dogmatics, ethics, and aesthetics but refuses to separate them into independent spheres. This means, fourth, that while the arts have a necessary freedom in order to express their creativity, they are also called to be responsible.

There has long been an interest in aesthetics amongst neo-Calvinists, and there is a growing interest today in theology and the arts within the life of Reformed churches and seminaries, especially in the United States. This is to be welcomed, affirmed, and more widely encouraged in those areas of Reformed presence where, perhaps for historical and missiological reasons, the arts have been neglected or opposed. But it is of vital importance that this interest be grounded in critical theological reflection. Otherwise there is a danger of losing theological integrity and coherence, degenerating on the one hand into an uncritical ecclesial kitsch or, on the other hand, conforming to the dictates of "high culture." My essay is an attempt to encourage such critical reflection and help overcome these dangers, at least in theory, not in order to curtail imagination and creativity but to set them free in the search for and service of truth, goodness, and beauty.

The juxtaposing of holiness and beauty in the title of my paper goes to the heart of Reformed theological aesthetics. Taken together, they refer to the righteous demand of God's reign and yet the gracious attraction of God's love; the wholly otherness of God's mystery and yet the redemptive splendor of that which has been revealed. This provides the distinct framework within which Reformed Christianity should consider its appropriation and appreciation of the arts. With this in mind, we explore three interconnected themes. The first is the nature of, and the relationship between, beauty and holiness; the second, the relationship between the Holy Spirit and human creativity; and the third, the relationship between sanctification, good taste, and social transformation.

## THE BEAUTY OF HOLINESS

Isaiah's call to be a prophet of social justice (Isaiah 6) was an "aesthetic moment" of intense vision and audition, of seeing and hearing. The awesome glory of

Yahweh's holiness was revealed to the startled worshiper with such power that it led directly to his personal transformation. When he later recounted the happening, Isaiah could tell of what he had seen and heard only in symbols and metaphors that stretch the imagination to breaking point. His vision of God's holy beauty enabled him to perceive reality in a totally new way, the reality of God, of himself, and of an unjust world. By contrast, he soon discovered in pursuing his new vocation as prophet of social righteousness that most of his hearers could neither see nor hear what God had commanded him to declare. They might have been able to appreciate the splendor of the Temple with aesthetic delight, but their eyes and ears were closed to the awesome beauty of God's holiness and the cries of the poor and oppressed.

There is an undoubted tension in the Old Testament between hearing God's call and God's command to do justice in the world[10] and seeing and worshiping Yahweh amid the splendor of the Temple.[11] Yet it is a creative tension, well expressed in the phrase "the beauty of holiness." The expression comes from Psalm 96:9 (KJV), which was sung during the ceremony of enthronement celebrating the New Year in the Temple in postexilic Jerusalem. It invites those who are worshiping to sing a new song to Yahweh and so declare "his glory among the nations"(96:3).[12] It reminds them that Yahweh is "the LORD . . . most worthy of praise," unlike the idols of the nations, for Yahweh is the creator of all things, and "might and beauty are in his sanctuary." It calls the worshiping throng to enter the Temple to bring an offering and worship Yahweh in "the beauty of holiness." And it speaks of the Lord who reigns as the one who "judges the people with equity" and who, when "he comes to judge the earth," will do so "with justice."

But what precisely does "the beauty of holiness" mean? The Hebrew is ambiguous, as can be discerned from the various renditions in English translations.[13] One reading emphasizes that the liturgical encounter between Yahweh and Isaiah occurred, in Walter Brueggemann's words, "in an environment of beauty, which makes communion possible and reflects Yahweh's own character."[14] But evangelical translators, who have been wary of any ritualistic aestheticism, place the emphasis not on a holy place or vestments but on "the splendor of God's holiness." This echoes the KJV rendering and finds expression in John Monsell's well-known nineteenth-century hymn, "Worship the Lord in the beauty of holiness," in which the offerings we are to bring are the "gold of obedience," "truth in its beauty," "love in its tenderness," and the "incense of lowliness."

The Reformed tradition has invariably drawn a distinction between worship in the Temple and worship in the Christian sanctuary, on the assumption that church worship is based on the synagogue rather than the Temple and is therefore quite different. While the prophetic word and its summation in the Decalogue have been strongly affirmed and often represented in decorative form, instructions regarding the Temple cultus have been disregarded or treated as matters of indifference (*adiaphora*). The Temple is the body in whom the Spirit dwells (1 Cor. 3:16; 6:19). True worship (*leitourgia*) has to do with the "living sacrifice" of a holy life (Rom. 12:1–2), not the right performance of a ritual, the design and furnishing of the sanctuary, or the splendor of priestly vestments. But we must be careful of positing a false dichotomy between Temple and church worship or assuming that the prophetic tradition regarded Temple worship and its splendor as unimportant.

What the prophetic tradition opposed was the hypocrisy of worship that basked in the splendor of the Temple but failed to recognize the beauty of God's holiness and its call to oppose ugly injustice, an aestheticism and piety unrelated to mercy and justice.[15] Beauty and holiness in the Hebrew Scriptures are taken together, so that the beauty of a holy life and the beauty of the holy place are both reflections of the beauty of the holy God. This is fundamental. Neither the sanctuary nor the priestly vestments, neither decorative art nor worshipers, have intrinsic holiness. Holiness is derived from God's holiness, and it is the beauty of God's holiness that makes them beautiful. God's beauty is uniquely God's. It is holy beauty. For this reason, as Karl Barth insisted, we cannot describe God's beauty on the basis of our own definition of what beauty might be, but only with reference to the form in which God's beauty is revealed both in creation and in redemption.[16] Even then, Barth insisted, we dare not visually *represent* the mystery of God's beauty revealed in Jesus Christ.[17] There can be no analogy! Not only would such images freeze our understanding of Christ within a particular context,[18] but even more, the beauty of God revealed in Christ is an alien beauty that judges all other forms of beauty. Hence Barth's plea to all Christian artists to "give up this unholy undertaking—for the sake of God's beauty."

This Barthian admonition is obviously related to the Second Commandment. If truth can be perverted into ideological dogmatism and goodness into self-righteous moralism, beauty is even more susceptible to idolatry because of its fascinating appeal and its apparent ability to satisfy human longing. Such Romantic aestheticism explains in part the Reformed reluctance to engage in theological aesthetics—but it also makes it imperative that we do so. Dogmatic systems and ethical codes cannot easily compete with the power of beauty in touching the heart and affections. But precisely for this reason, many who think they possess beauty are deluded into assuming that they have grasped the holy.[19] Augustine recognized this when he wrote of the power of beauty to allure and unite us to the things we love.[20] For just as beauty has the power to attract us to the worship of God, so too it has the power to seduce us into fashioning and worshiping false gods.

In this regard, there is an important connection between Reformed theology and those engaged in cultural studies today who are concerned with the production and manipulation of mass-media images and icons. We need no reminding that we are daily bombarded with such images and of their power to obfuscate reality. We look and look but, as both Jesus and Isaiah observed, we do not really see. The motivation of genuine iconoclasm is precisely to break down these images, made more tantalizing by their apparent beauty, so that we can see again. The prophetic cry against injustice sometimes implies or even promotes the destruction of national icons, as, for example, in the burning of a national flag. Indeed, art, in its endeavor to help us see differently, is often icon-oclastic, reacting against images and symbols associated with dehumanizing ide-ologies and powers.

As necessary as iconoclasm sometimes is in a world saturated by false images, ill-informed iconoclasm—the iconoclasm of book burners and art destroyers—can also prove destructive and disastrous for society, contributing to its oppres-sive ugliness rather than redeeming it. The motives of iconoclasts are often shaped by greed and a lust for power. Moreover, the destruction of idols does not prevent the children of iconoclasts from creating new images that may be just as idolatrous. In that great citadel of Prussian Protestantism, the Berliner Dom, the massive sanctuary is surrounded not by images of the apostles, as in St. Peter's Square, but by images of the Protestant reformers and princes! Barth's radical critique of such cultural Protestantism is an authentic part of our Reformed heritage.

Yet it was none other than Barth, whose "No" to Hellenism was at times almost as loud as his "Yes" to the gospel, who warned us against the dangers of disparaging Hellenism in the name of biblical religion.[21] In this, as in other mat-ters, the "No" of negation was to be followed at the appropriate moment by the "Yes" of affirmation. In Barth's words: "The imagination which created the Homeric Olympus and its inhabitants is one of the strongest proofs of the fact that the heart of man is evil from his youth. Yet for all that the Greeks were able to reveal the human heart, to show what humanity is in itself."[22] In Barth's dis-cussion of Hellenism and biblical revelation, of *erôs* and *agapê*, we face the ques-tion of the relationship between the Christ of faith and the muse of Mount Parnassus, between the Holy Spirit and the spirit of human creativity. For is it not true that the artists are often those who show us "what humanity is in itself" and thereby help us in knowing ourselves and therefore knowing God?

## HOLY SPIRIT AND HUMAN CREATIVITY

God, Calvin argued, is far greater than human thought can imagine or human beings can represent through their image making. Seeing that God has no simi-larity to those shapes by means of which people attempt to represent him, all attempts to depict him are an impudent affront to his majesty and glory.[23] On this all Christians would surely agree. But does this apply to representations of Jesus Christ as well, as Barth and other Reformed theologians have argued?

The issue must surely be approached dialectically. There is always the need for an iconoclastic "No" to certain images of Christ, whether these be images com-municated through the words of a preacher or the art of a painter or sculptor. The Aryan Christ of the Nazi apologists, for example, must be resisted, however presented. So the eighth-century Byzantine iconoclasts were exercising a neces-sary critical theological responsibility. But they were also wrong in rejecting icons in principle. In this regard the iconophiles rightly defended their position on the basis of the incarnation. "The Word became flesh" and therefore became an image. There is no way whereby we can truly know something of the mystery of God incarnate in Christ other than in terms of images that relate to our present reality and experience. God, as Calvin emphasized, accommodates to our ability to grasp and understand.

If artists through the centuries had taken Barth's advice, some of the greatest artistic and profoundly Christian masterpieces, from Russian icons, through the murals in the Sistine Chapel, to Pier Paolo Pasolini's film *The Gospel according to St. Matthew*, would never have been created. Neither would so much art in contemporary Asia or sub-Saharan Africa through which Christ has become culturally represented.[24] This would undoubtedly be to the impoverishment of the human spirit as well as to the detriment of the life and witness of the church. Despite Barth's categorical "No" to representations of Christ, a "Yes" sneaks in, as, for example, in his deep appreciation for Matthias Grünewald's *Crucifixion* (the Isenheim altarpiece), which so profoundly portrays the redemptive suffering of Christ. Can we deny that the Spirit is at work in such works of art, pointing us, with John the Baptist, to the Lamb of God? The issue is surely whether or not the Word and the Spirit agree that this, indeed, is Jesus the Christ.

But let us go beyond the problem of the representation of the divine as such, whether the mystery of God or of God incarnate, and consider the work of the Spirit in artistic creativity more broadly. For Calvin, the Holy Spirit was the source of genuine artistic creativity, and artistic gifts sometimes flowered more brilliantly among those who were not believers.[25] All arts, sculpture and painting included, come from God and can bring pleasure.[26] Calvin's categorical rejection of the gods of Olympus and any semblance of idolatry was not a condemnation of the arts as such but of the attempt to represent the majesty of God. Thus works of art proscribed in the sanctuary might be quite appropriate in the public square. Images in secular places are not harmful; even idols kept in such places are not worshiped.[27]

The best of the Puritans likewise did not object to the arts as such (consider the poets Edmund Spenser, Philip Sidney, John Milton, and Andrew Marvell); nor did they lack appreciation of the beautiful or refuse on occasion to pay their respects to the spirit of the muses. What they objected to was ostentation and adornment that distracted from the dignity and simplicity of true worship and therefore authentic Christian living. They also objected, with Calvin, to any attempt by artists to usurp the role of God as creator.

The true artist, however, is not one who seeks to compete with God as creator but someone whose creativity is a painful yet joyful response to God's providence and grace. Hence Barth's comments about the "incomparable Mozart," whose music provides "food and drink" for the Christian, and for which even the epithet "beautiful" is inadequate.[28] Genuine artistic creation is a gift, a Spirit-inspired construction that breaks open that which is hidden so that it may manifest itself, even if only for a brief moment.

Nonetheless, the form and manifestation of the "beauty that saves" is a strange and alien beauty that challenges and transforms all our assumptions. So it is only when aesthetics is liberated from the tyranny of superficial and facile images of the beautiful that it can begin to understand the beauty of God and its redemptive power amid the harsh reality of the world. Indeed, the beauty of God that is hidden in Jesus the crucified Messiah and supremely veiled from sight in the ugliness of the cross can be discerned only through the gift of the Spirit. It is through the Spirit that we are enabled to see and hear what is manifest in God's revelation in Jesus Christ. Moreover, it is through the Spirit that the beauty of God in the form of Jesus Christ becomes the power that attracts and transforms, bringing us through the painfulness of death and rebirth into conformity with the image of Christ (Gal. 4:19). And it is through the same Spirit that God inspires human creativity to reflect both the ugly pain of the world and the beauty of redemption.

In her delightful essay on "Artful Theology," Sara Maitland convincingly argues that the renewal of the church as a transforming community in society is related to the extent to which it takes seriously the creative arts. Her reason is profoundly theological: "because we create in this particular and conscious way only in the light of the creative power of our God." In other words, artistic creativity not only is God-given but is one of the main ways whereby the power of God is unleashed, awakening both a thirst for justice and a hunger for beauty. She continues: "Any movement for social change requires a revolution of the imagination."[29] A challenge facing the church if it is serious about its own renewal and social transformation, then, is how to harness the creative energy and insight of local artists.

One of the Reformed theologians of the early twentieth century who recognized the necessary dialectic in which the church says "No" to certain aspects of art and yet joyously affirms art and aesthetic sensibility as a gift of the Spirit was P. T. Forsyth. Although sometimes referred to as a "Barth before Barth," Forsyth was more positive in his embrace of Hellenism and in his desire to discern Christ on Mount Parnassus. And even though historical veracity is sometimes distorted by his rhetoric, he provides flashes of insight that take us forward in our quest for a Reformed aesthetic:

> In Greece it was Art that destroyed Religion; in Europe it was Religion that destroyed Art. In Greece, the people, in the name of Beauty, ceased to believe; in Christendom, the people, in the name of Truth, ceased to delight and enjoy. In Greece, Faith sank as taste spread; in Christian Europe, Faith rose and taste decayed. . . . In Greece the Imagination destroyed the Conscience, in Europe the Conscience paralysed the Imagination.[30]

There is obviously a fundamental difference between art and religion. Art enhances faith, but it is not a replacement for faith. Art provides a vehicle for the Spirit, but it is not the power of the Spirit. Hence the aesthetic "peril to religion," which derives from what Forsyth calls its "monopoly of the feelings." Whether in literature or art, impression "is mistaken for regeneration, and to move men is prized as highly as to change them." The fundamental error—and this is of particular significance for our theme—"is the submersion of the ethical element, of the centrality of the conscience, and the authority of the holy."[31] Art and religion need each other, but faith cannot find an escape from moral challenge in beauty; neither can beauty find an escape in faith without moral commitment. For just as beauty has the power to attract us to the worship of God, so too it has the power to seduce us into fashioning and worshiping false gods.[32]

Nonetheless, great art speaks to the soul, and while it may oust religion, it can also save religion from becoming closed and hardened. Faith without a sense of beauty, or religion severed from imagination and overengrossed with public and practical affairs, leaves us with "a drought in our own souls."[33] It no longer evokes a sense of wonder. Art, in fact, is "not a luxury" but "a necessity of human nature." For this reason, no "religion can be a true religion if it does not encourage great art."[34] Acknowledging that much Western art had lost touch with its religious source, advocating the holiness of beauty rather than the beauty of holiness, Forsyth nevertheless declared that while beauty might not be *the* way to God, it is *a* way. We "shall not go far in a true sense of the beauty of holiness without gaining a deeper sense of the holiness of beauty."[35] That deeper sense brings together what the New Testament refers to as sanctification and what aesthetics calls good taste. Growing in holiness includes developing a sense of beauty.

## SANCTIFICATION, GOOD TASTE, AND TRANSFORMATION

Frank Burch Brown has helpfully drawn our attention to the relationship between sin and bad taste, on the one hand, and sanctification and good taste, on the other. Aesthetic discernment or good taste, he argues, is a key element in religion.[36] There is, as illustrated in the call of Isaiah, "an analogy between aesthetic experience and the experience of the holy or divine."[37] Aesthetic excellence, from a Christian perspective, is "part of the glorification and enjoyment of God that is possible through the moral life."[38] This has seldom been recognized in Christian tradition, where bad taste is certainly not considered a deadly or even a venial sin. Nor is it normally condemned as a hindrance to sanctification or spiritual maturity. Impeccable "taste is hardly deemed to be one of the 'fruits of the spirit.'"[39] Yet for the church to acquiesce in tasteless shoddiness will not inspire its members to creative expressions of response to the gospel in the world.

Christian formation does not take place only through teaching (truth) or example (goodness) but also through the cultivation of a sense of taste for what is genuinely beautiful in a world of competing images and ugliness. Yet, as Brown indicates,

> [t]he possibility that bad taste may be a *moral* liability is suggested in fact by the quite traditional notion that sin—which is not only wrong but also profoundly ugly—looks alluring to the unwary, whereas virtue – which is not only right but also profoundly beautiful—frequently appears drab at first

sight. It follows that failure to distinguish beauty from counterfeit can lead to moral error. Moral and aesthetic discernment often go hand in hand.[40]

This has been supremely true of Calvinist aesthetics in which, as Donald Davie observed with regard to Huguenot and Dutch Reformed architecture, "everything breathes *simplicity, sobriety,* and *measure*"[41]—qualities that reflect a particular understanding of God and the world in which truth, morality, and beauty belong together.

One of Brown's representative types of bad taste is the philistine, whose sin is the failure to take delight, whether in God or in anything artistic.[42] Philistinism is "the antithesis *par excellence* of aesthetic behaviour." It is not simply vulgarity; it represents, as Adorno noted, "indifference to or hatred of art."[43] This may be rationalized on the basis of moral commitment or a concern to oppose idolatry and maintain purity. As such, philistinism is perhaps the sin most commonly associated with Calvinists and Puritans. Taken to an extreme, philistinism results in iconoclasm, the uprooting of that which does not conform to our image of the good and true. This concern for moral and dogmatic purity plagued the Dutch Reformed Church in South Africa during the apartheid years, resulting in the censorship of those artists who stepped out of line. If art does not fit your criteria, and especially if it offends your religious convictions, then you declare it idolatrous and set about its exclusion or even destruction.

Philistinism expresses itself in many different forms. For example, a lack of care and respect for the environment may arise out of the failure to take delight in nature, that "beautiful theater" according to Calvin. Philistinism is also the failure to appreciate the artistic creativity of people and cultures different from our own. Good taste is not the sole possession of a particular ethnic community or some company of the culturally elite; nor is bad taste a characteristic of those who do not belong there. But there are other forms of philistinism that are perplexingly problematic because they seem to be so morally correct. For example, can a society afford to sponsor works of art when many of its citizens eke out their lives in poverty? Like earlier Cistercian reformers, Calvin was concerned about the ostentatious decoration of churches not least because of the misuse of money that should be given to the poor. The dehumanizing of the "image of God" in men and women was as serious as the idolatry of placing sacred images in the sanctuary. Should not world poverty force us all to become aesthetic "philistines" in the pursuit of economic justice? Is this not more important for sanctification than the cultivation of aesthetic judgment and good taste?

On the contrary, the danger of allowing philistinism to set the agenda for sanctification would be disastrous for the long-term well-being of society. Christoph Gestrich's exposition of the Christian doctrine of sin confirms the insight of D. H. Lawrence that people need beauty and not just bread. When "things no longer have any splendor," Gestrich writes, "their destruction is imminent." He goes on to say: "People who are headed for destruction are first deprived of their honor, stripped of their rights, and their outward appearance takes on a pathetic, ugly form."[44] If, as Brown insists, "moral and aesthetic discernment often go hand in hand,"[45] moral striving and the struggle for justice cannot be separated from the sanctification of our aesthetic sensibility, that is, with the development of good taste. Good taste is that spiritual capacity which enables us to appreciate the difference between the genuine and the ersatz, between false beauty and true beauty, between kitsch that debases and popular art that challenges and inspires. Good taste helps us to know the difference between an extravagance that is unjust and the creation of splendor that humanizes, restores dignity, evokes hope, and thus contributes to renewal and transformation.

The transformative power of art does not lie in any overt political content or didactic intention but precisely in its aesthetic form and creative character. Art exercises its critical power by being art, by simply being there.[46] Yet this is not apolitical, for the necessity of art's autonomy derives from, and is dependent on, its ability to stand in opposition to society. "Art," Adorno insists, "will live on only as long as it has the power to resist society."[47] The "great artist," Monroe Beardsley once wrote, "is always exploring new perspectives, inventing intense new regional qualities, putting things together in hitherto unheard-of ways; and if what he makes is good, it will be the enemy of some established good that is not quite as good."[48] Thus, some of the most creative artists are those who are antiestablishment, purposely choosing to be on the "outside" because of the stifling character of society. Public outcries against their work, censorship by officialdom, and even death threats often result. In telling the story of the early development of black art in South Africa, Elza Miles speaks of art as an "intervention" that introduces a deeper discourse into the public square, resisting structures of power that dehumanize. Such art intervention may "provoke outrage, as in the case of the art of AIDS activism," yet it is essential for the well-being of democratic society.[49] This highlights the social significance of such art compared to the sterility of much that is religiously or politically correct, and therefore of the importance for the church to be sensitive in its response.

There are, of course, boundaries to what is appropriate art in both the sanctuary and the public square. Creativity can be abused. Works that may, for example, encourage sectarian violence, racism, or sexual abuse are clearly inappropriate. However, the church should be careful not to act as a self-righteous but ill-informed moral guardian of aesthetic and artistic creativity. It should recognize that many so-called antisocial works of art are a form of protest against the ills, the meaninglessness, and the blind hypocrisies of society, rather than support for them. There is far more danger to society in the seductive art of certain kinds of advertising that promote questionable values than there is in the work of those artists who employ the tactics of shock to awaken social conscience. But none of this implies that Christians should not exercise critical judgment on the products of human creativity when these warrant critique. Artists, like anyone else, are called to use their gifts responsibly.

Art in itself cannot change society, but good art, whatever its form, helps us both individually and corporately to perceive reality in a new way, and by so doing, it opens up possibilities of transformation. In this way art has the potential to change both our personal and our corporate consciousness and perception, challenging perceived reality and enabling us to remember what was best in the past even as it evokes fresh images that serve transformation in the present. This it does through its ability to evoke imagination and wonder, causing us to pause and reflect and thereby opening up the possibility of changing our perception and ultimately our lives. But art—and here, in conclusion, I return to my main theme—cannot fulfill its transformative function if the expression of beauty is excluded as a goal.

Herbert Marcuse spoke of the beautiful as representative of the pleasure principle rebelling against the principles of domination and death. "The work of art," he wrote, "speaks the liberating language, invokes the liberating images of the subordination of death and destruction to the will to live." This is "the emancipatory element in aesthetic affirmation."[50] So it is that the beautiful serves transformation by supplying images that contradict the inhuman and thus provides alternative, transforming images to those of oppression.[51] From a Christian perspective, the supreme image that contradicts the inhuman and, in doing so, becomes the icon of redemption is that of the incarnate, crucified, and risen Christ. So it is not surprising that artists through the centuries have sought to represent that alien beauty as a counter to the ugliness of injustice. We are not redeemed by art or by beauty alone, but by the holy beauty that is revealed in Christ and, through the Spirit, evokes wonder and stirs our imagination.

Chapter 2

# The Theology and Ethics of Martin Luther King Jr.: Contributions to Christian Thought and Practice

*Peter J. Paris*

In 1980, Dr. Gayraud S. Wilmore gave a series of lectures at San Francisco Theological Seminary, which were published later under the title *Black and Presbyterian: The Heritage and the Hope.* The purpose of that book was to demonstrate how a small number of African Americans in the Presbyterian Church had persevered in that context for one and a half centuries as the bearers of the African American Christian heritage. While some had joined that predominantly white denomination because they had come to believe that only there could they find authentic Christianity, many others had become members out of convenience alone. Wilmore's purpose in the book was to encourage the latter, to correct the former, and to inform the whole denomination about the theological meaning of the ethnic particularity of Jesus of Nazareth and the normative implications of his ethnicity for the many diverse races and ethnic groups around the world. Hence he argued that before the message of God's kingdom could be proclaimed to all the peoples of the world, its incarnation in one person in a particular time and place was necessary:

> The message of the Kingdom of God had to begin somewhere before it could be disseminated everywhere. It had to originate in the life, death, and

resurrection of a particular person, in a particular time and place, and among a particular people, before it could become the universal Word of Life for the redemption of the world.[1]

Because of God's affirmation of Jesus' ethnic particularity, African Americans gradually came to believe that normative humanity was not any one racial or ethnic form but many. In other words, they discerned that God had created a diversity of human beings—male and female, black and white, Jews and Gentiles of many nations speaking numerous languages—and that none of them was superior to any of the others. That discovery made all the difference in their self-understanding. Thus, Wilmore wrote:

> We all want to be taken for what we are—creatures made in the image of God—and not have that which is a part of us, our color, race, nationality, or gender cast aside as if it were only an unfortunate excrescence and that the pure, undefiled you or me were hidden somewhere inside.[2]

Wilmore argued persuasively that the principal focus of the African American Christian heritage had arisen out of suffering and that its primary focus both during and after slavery was the quest for freedom and dignity, which African American Christians believed constituted their divine calling:

> Without an emphasis on freedom and liberation the Black Christian Tradition is without its anchor in Jesus Christ, for he is the liberator *par excellence* and it is because of the freedom Blacks found in him that their churches were called into existence.[3]

During the antebellum period, many notable African American Presbyterian clergy applied the education they had received from the predominantly Anglo-American church to the task of persistently seeking the eradication of racial oppression both from the church and from the nation at large. Among the most notable of these black Presbyterian prophets were Samuel Cornish, editor of the first black newspaper, *Freedom's Journal*, and founder of the First Colored Presbyterian Church in New York (1822); Theodore S. Wright, the first black graduate from Princeton Theological Seminary (1828); Henry Highland Garnett; J. W. C. Pennington; and Francis Grimke.[4]

Wilmore also presented a brief synopsis of the many and varied historical struggles within the denomination for racial justice: struggles that were led by courageous African American clergy, that continued throughout the twentieth century, and that eventually culminated in the work of a group founded in 1963 that called itself the Concerned Presbyterians and that was the precursor of the Black Presbyterians United, a caucus founded in 1968. Wilmore concluded his analysis with the judgment that black Presbyterians came of age within the denomination during the 1960s. He sums up his estimation of the mutual, enduring benefits that whites and blacks derived from their long encounter with the words of Dr. Leland Stanford Cozart, the first black president of Barber-Scotia College, who wisely said:

Because of the Presbyterian Church, the Negro in America today is infinitely the richer in body, mind and spirit; because of the Negro, the Presbyterian Church is immeasurably more responsive to human needs, more brotherly and more Christian.[5]

## TWO FORMS OF CHRISTIAN SPIRITUALITY

Two opposing types of Christian spirituality have long endured in the Presbyterian Church, shaped by different understandings of racial justice: the one Euro-American and the other African American. These two forms of spirituality encountered each other in the church nearly two centuries ago, and they have lived together in varying degrees of conflict ever since. Unlike the Euro-American type of Christianity, the Christianity of African peoples in America has been based on a doctrine of humanity that is inclusive of all peoples. That is to say, it is nonracist. As such, African American Christianity has represented a novel movement in the history of Western Christianity. No other Christian association among Western peoples can lay claim to such origins. Some have notable histories of opposing the enslavement of African peoples, yet it would be erroneous to assume that their opposition to slavery invariably implied a fundamental belief in the equality of all humans. The eventual institutionalization of their belief in a common humanity constitutes the unique contribution of African American Christianity to the Western world.

Instead of bolting from all the predominantly Euro-American Christian churches, a remnant of African Americans remained in each of them. Eventually, they laid claim to those churches, including the Presbyterian Church, as their inheritance also, and not that of Euro-Americans alone. In the early 1960s, a significant number of Euro-Americans in general and Presbyterians in particular were transformed as they gradually embraced the spiritual vision of the African American Christian heritage as interpreted and proclaimed by Martin Luther King Jr. That experience enabled a significant portion of the Presbyterian Church to depart from what Wilmore called its hypocritical past by uniting its normative teaching about racial justice with commensurate moral practices in the public arena. Thus, Wilmore succinctly summed up the challenge of the Black Christian Tradition with the following question:

> The issue for the Black Church may be put in these terms: "How can Black Christians use the history, culture, and experience of their historic struggle for freedom, something that is distinctively theirs, to enhance the proclamation of the gospel of Jesus Christ and the manifestation of his power to transform not only Black humanity but the whole human race?"[6]

That question implies a major challenge to all religious and political communities everywhere: a challenge that was embraced fully by Martin Luther King Jr., who lived and died as an exemplar of the African American Christian tradition.

Let us now explore the salient elements in the theology and ethics of the African American Christian tradition as embodied in the thought and practice of Martin Luther King Jr. The purpose of this analysis is to invite all who stand in the Reformed tradition to assess the extent to which they can embrace the African American Christian tradition. That assessment will determine the extent to which the two forms of spirituality can be united. Short of such a union, the prospects of fruitful relations between the two traditions will remain problematic.

## THE THEOLOGY AND ETHICS
## OF MARTIN LUTHER KING JR.

Primarily a minister of the gospel of Jesus Christ and secondarily a social reformer, King's vocation was to clarify the nature of America's race problem and to inspire his people to struggle for justice, guided by the vision of a just God who was incarnated in Jesus of Nazareth. Most important, King sought to give practical expression to the teachings of Jesus by adopting the strategy of non-violent resistance, which, he insisted, was inspired by the Sermon on the Mount, regulated by the principle of love (*agapê*), and demonstrated best of all in the twentieth century by the public practices of Mahatma Gandhi.

Clearly, King's sacred vocation of liberating his people from racial oppression was coupled with the similar aim of liberating his nation from its captivity to the same evil force that had consumed its energies for several centuries. Gradually, the logic of his struggle for racial justice would lead him to extend that concern to other forms of human oppression, such as apartheid in South Africa, worldwide poverty, and American militarism, all of which, along with racism, he viewed as interrelated phenomena. Like Jesus, King taught his followers how to reconcile themselves to their enemies in the actual pursuit of racial justice. In doing so, his ministry issued in a social movement that, in fleeting moments, mirrored some of the marks of the *new creation* that Christ promised to inaugurate.

In King's thought there is no discussion of God in abstraction from the human condition, and similarly, there is no fundamental discussion of the human condition apart from God. In fact, discussion of both God and the human situation is always in the context of some particular struggle for justice between races, classes, or nations. In short, he claimed that there can be no rightful discussion of God apart from ethics, which is the art of enhancing the quality of our common life.

In keeping with the scriptural teaching of John 3:16, King believed that God's love is for the world and its redemption. Throughout his formative years, he had been nurtured in that belief through the symbiotic relationship of his family, his church, and his alma mater, Morehouse College. In each of those contexts the relatedness of religion to cultural and societal affairs was taken for granted; such was also the case with the graduate schools where he studied, Crozer Theological Seminary and Boston University School of Theology.

In all of King's thought, speeches, and writings, no theme was more pervasive than that of God's sovereignty and the obligations that follow from obedience and loyalty to God's purpose for the world. I contend that every significant concept pervading his works derives from his understanding of God. Those concepts include nonviolent resistance, love, hope, justice, power, human dignity, reconciliation, responsibility, freedom, morality, and redemptive suffering. Certainly, King stood in a tradition in which God was seen on the one hand as intimately related to the human community by constantly challenging it "to love mercy, do justice, and walk humbly with their God" while on the other hand constantly correcting and forgiving the community for its wrongdoing, unfaithfulness, and hard-heartedness.

Undoubtedly, King's theology was in continuity with the Jewish and Christian traditions. He believed in a God who not only created the world but is an active agent in the world, striving to redeem it from its own folly. Thus, his belief in God the Liberator and God the Redeemer, respectively, integrates the two cardinal theological doctrines of Judaism and Christianity. Moreover, God's justice is implied by both traditions.

To show the relatedness of King's theology to historical contexts, let us approach our subject by a brief examination of the presuppositions that underlie the worship experiences of Jews and Christians. In this exercise, we will see how King embraced the presuppositions of both Jews and Christians while drawing on the resources of the African American Christian tradition as a necessary corrective to the anthropology affirmed by those traditions.

## God as Liberator

First of all, it is important to note that every experience of Jewish worship is an act of communal remembrance relative to the wondrous act of God, who, in the beginning of their history, initiated and guided action that resulted in the Israelites' deliverance from bondage. The act of worship signifies the worshipers reaffirmation of their covenant with God: their vocation to be a special people endowed with a special mission of faithfulness to the God of their deliverance through religious devotion and habitual acts of mercy and justice in the world.

King drew heavily on the exodus event as both a religious source and a political symbol of inspiration and hope. Consonant with the tradition of many preeminent African American religious leaders, King viewed himself as called by God to be a prophet, that is, God's spokesperson for justice. The words he uttered in his final sermon, the night before his assassination, have gained a measure of immortality because his declaration that he had seen the promised land typified his prophetic self-awareness. For King, the exodus was the paramount historical evidence that God is in control of history, guiding it to its true end, and that the victory of good over evil ultimately is assured. In that sense, he believed that goodness is at the center of history. That is what he meant by his frequent references to justice being at the center of the universe, evidenced by God's presence as Creator and Sustainer of all goodness. Also, "The Death of Evil upon the Seashore," the title of one of his sermons, was another vivid reminder that God is actively engaged at the center of the universe in a perennial struggle against evil. In fact, King believed that the phrase "God is Spirit" means "God is freedom." Consequently, the nature of the *imago dei* in humankind means *freedom*, not reason, as so many have supposed. Thus, the struggle for freedom is the struggle for the restoration of true humanity, or the *imago dei* in humankind. That struggle implies a partnership with God, who determined in creation human beings' true nature and final end.

## God as Redeemer

Second, it is important to note that every act of Christian worship presupposes the wondrous act of God's incarnation in the person of Jesus of Nazareth, whose life of perfect faith, hope, and love led to his crucifixion and, subsequently, the final demonstration of God's sovereignty over all things, including death itself: namely, the resurrection. Thus, Christian worship is always an act of grateful remembrance of God's redemptive act in history, of the availability of God's grace in the present, and of God's eschatological promise of fulfillment in the future. Further, in many of the free-church traditions, Christian worship presupposes God's personal and interactive relationship with humankind. This is manifested by the experience that King had while alone in his kitchen, late at night, after the bombing of his home, when his wife and daughter narrowly escaped death. That occasion constituted a conversion experience for him, one in which he accepted God's call to a prophetic vocation.[7]

## God as Liberator and Redeemer

Third, the African American experience of worship presupposes God's wondrous act of solidarity with enslaved Africans in America, who spent three centuries as chattel slaves and another century as racial pariahs. While in the cauldron of slavery, and by some miracle, these enslaved people discerned an understanding of God that contradicted the theology that had been promulgated among them by their slaveholders and the latter's preachers. This new understanding revealed a God who affirmed the dignity of African peoples as created in the image of God and, hence, condemned those who viewed them as an inferior race. Dr. King had been nurtured in that understanding, which had been concealed from the eyes of Euro-Americans by the racially segregated pattern of their social world.

Contrary to the racist tradition of slaveholders and racial segregationists, African Americans had kept alive a heritage in their churches that unified their theology and anthropology. That is, they believed that God had created one species of human beings and not two. Within their segregated confines, enslaved Africans and their descendents expressed their devotion to the liberating God in song and music, prayer and testimony, dancing and preaching, as well as in various forms of resistance to the many acts of dehumanization perpetrated on them. Under the conditions of slavery, African Christians had initiated various occasions for clandestine worship as alternatives to the liturgical practices of their slave masters. Most important, those occasions signaled an alternative understanding of the nature of God and of humankind. The miracle that occurred was the creation of new songs while in bondage: songs of sorrow, pain, suffering, faith, courage, and hope; songs that integrated the experience of suffering with their faith in a liberating sovereign God. In 1900, James Weldon Johnson caught that spirit in his immortal anthem of sorrow and hope, known today as the African American national anthem:

> Lift every voice and sing,
> Till earth and heaven ring,
> Ring with the harmonies of liberty;
> Let our rejoicing rise,
> High as the listening skies,
> Let it resound loud as the rolling sea.
> Sing a song full of the faith that the dark past has taught us,
> Sing a song full of the hope that the present has brought us;
> Facing the rising sun of our new day begun,
> Let us march on till victory is won.
>
> Stony the road we trod,
> Bitter the chastening rod,
> Felt in the days when hope unborn had died;
> Yet with a steady beat,
> Have not our weary feet
> Come to the place for which our fathers sighed?
> We have come over a way that with tears has been watered,
> We have come, treading our path thru the blood of the slaughtered;
> Out of the gloomy past,
> Till now we stand at last
> Where the white gleam of our bright star is cast.
>
> God of our weary years,
> God of our silent tears,
> Thou who hast brought us thus far on the way,
> Thou who hast by Thy might,
> Led us into the light,
> Keep us forever in the path we pray.
> Lest our feet stray from the places, our God, where we met Thee,
> Lest, our hearts drunk with the wine of the world, we forget Thee;
> Shadowed beneath Thy hand,
> May we forever stand,
> True to our God,
> True to our native land.[8]

As stated above, King had been well nurtured in the theology and ethics of the African American Christian tradition, the basic principle of which I call "the parenthood of God and the kinship of all peoples." That principle was institutionalized in the independent Black Church movement of the late eighteenth century and was normative for all of King's thought and practice. Thus, the primacy of one God and one humankind has been the predominant worldview among African American Christianity from the beginning of its history up to the present day. Their discovery of biblical support for such a belief enabled African Americans to embrace the Christian faith and view its essence as a principle of criticism on racist thought and practice.

Similarly, African Americans have always been deeply impressed with the profound biblical messages of freedom and dignity that pervade the utterances of the Hebrew prophets, including Jesus of Nazareth. Most important, they have been greatly moved by the prophetic concern for the poor, the outcasts, and the oppressed—concerns that issued in strong condemnations of every form of social and religious injustice. Hence, all forms of worship in the African American Christian tradition presuppose God's condemnation of human bondage and oppression. That was the Christian theology that enslaved Africans embraced on these shores. It was the impetus that motivated Richard Allen and others to remove themselves from the segregated sections of white churches and to found their own churches, in order to institutionalize the gospel of freedom and justice for all regardless of race or social circumstance. It was also the motivation for women such as Sojourner Truth, Harriet Tubman, Jarena Lee, Zilpha Elaw, Ida Wells Barnett, Mary Church Terrell, and Nannie Burroughs in their courageous quests for human dignity and social justice. African Americans' prophetic criticism of white slaveholding Christianity and the subsequent institutionalization of a nonracist anthropology in their churches constituted uniqueness in American religious history. No Euro-American institution, Christian or otherwise, can lay claim to a similar nonracist tradition.

This new form of Christianity, institutionalized in the African American churches, portrayed God as liberator and redeemer of all oppressed peoples and opposed to all who were bent on creating and maintaining structures of oppression. Henceforth, God became for African Americans the ultimate ground for their fundamental understanding of human nature and history. Further, with few exceptions, the equality of all people under God has been and continues to be the fundamental principle of African American associational life, both within and ouside their churches. Most important, African Americans have sought to bear witness to this tradition in the predominantly white denominations in which they have been called to participate.

Faithfulness to the black Christian belief that God is friend of all oppressed peoples has saved blacks from falling victim to fatalism and despair. In fact, that faith has provided them with theological grounds for the expectation that suffering does not last forever. Because they believed that God was on their side, they felt destined to be victorious. Thus, Dr. King could say that even if he were killed, the movement itself could not be stopped because "God is on our side." Expectation of a better world of equality and freedom for all—a world where every person would be enabled to flourish in spite of natural diversity—is commensurate with the eschatological hope in the eventual sovereign reign of God. This is the "beloved community" on behalf of which all King's endeavors were concentrated. All of this was implicit in his "I Have a Dream" speech, which was the twentieth century's most celebrated rhetorical expression of the African American Christian tradition.

King's theological position was deeply rooted in the biblical tradition, yet he drew upon the insights of philosophy, social science, literature, and general historical experience whenever those findings supported particular biblical understandings of God and humanity. Accordingly, he considered the Declaration of Independence, the U.S. Constitution, the Bill of Rights, and human conscience as sources for ethical judgment insofar as they were commensurate with the biblical understanding of God and humanity. His doctrine of God was the final normative standard. Similarly, he could say in his first book, *Stride toward Freedom: The Montgomery Story*, that the philosophy of the movement was the Sermon on the Mount (i.e., Christian love) and not primarily what many were saying it was, namely, nonviolent resistance, noncooperation, or passive resistance. Rather, he insisted that Jesus was the inspiration of the movement, nonviolent resistance the method that was regulated by the ideal of Christian love. In other words, he taught that God is love and the goal that love seeks is the restoration of community. Nonviolent resistance facilitates that goal. It is the means to the end, commensurate with the end but not synonymous with that end. King also wrote in that same book that his two favorite Scripture passages were Paul's 1 Corinthians 13, "Now faith, hope, and love abide" and the passage "Then came Peter to him and said, Lord, how oft shall my brother sin against me, and I forgive him? till seven times? Jesus saith unto him, I say not unto thee, Until seven times: but, Until seventy times seven" (Matt.18:22, KJV). His ethical norm of forgiveness derived from the cross where Jesus died forgiving his enemies, those who were putting him to death.

Now, King was not so naive as to believe that all African American churches were equally faithful to their prophetic calling. Rather, he repeatedly said that there were three ways to deal with oppression: (1) acquiescence, (2) violent revolt, and (3) nonviolent resistance. Concerning the first, he was fully aware that the lifestyles of vast numbers of African Americans and their churches exemplified acquiescence. Repeatedly, he contended that those who cooperate with evil are as guilty as those who perpetrate it. Concerning the second style, he was emphatic that violence breeds violence and is contrary to God's design for humankind. Third, his strong advocacy for nonviolent resistance seemed to him altogether right because it was commensurate with all the redemptive values implied in the life and teachings of Jesus and his eschatological vision of the "beloved community."

Let us hasten to add that King's prophetic challenge was not to whites alone but also to blacks—those who were prone to acquiesce and those who advocated the use of violence. Time and time again, he was pleased to speak about what he called the "New Negro," who symbolized all those who embraced the vision of the beloved community, affirmed the philosophy of nonviolent resistance, and resolved not ever to accept the conditions that rob people of their freedom and dignity.

## THE PROVIDENCE OF GOD

King believed implicitly in the providence of God, which is another cardinal doctrine in the African American Christian tradition. God as almighty sovereign guide protects the universe like a loving parent and is always available to support and protect us both individually and collectively. Hence, God is viewed as the source of all goodness and the ground of all ethics. This awareness of King and his followers constituted the primary source of their courage and perseverance from the days of the Montgomery bus boycott onward. *Stride toward Freedom* is replete with such testimony.

King also believed that because God created human beings with bodies, and since the body and the soul are integrally united, Christians should not ignore bodily needs; the condition of the soul is largely dependent on the condition of the body. Similarly, he argued that the Christian church should not ignore social problems that threaten the well-being of God's creation. Thus, in this respect, he reaffirmed Karl Marx's critique of religion as the opiate of the people.[9]

## THE PROBLEM OF THEODICY

In keeping with the faith of his ancestors, King believed that humans are not alone in the universe, not cut off from the creative source of their being. Rather, that divine source is constantly active in protecting and leading the whole of creation to its rightful destiny. This does not mean that God prevents human beings from experiencing evil (i.e., that which is contrary to their well-being) but rather that God is present as a constant source of help when needed. Thus, God does not control the universe like a puppeteer, because that would necessarily rob human beings of their freedom and, hence, destroy their humanity. God is very consistent, preventing humans neither from doing nor from encountering evil. We meet the problem of theodicy in this discussion: "Why does God allow evil to thrive?" or "Why does God allow the just to suffer?" For King and the tradition in which he was raised, the personal experience of God's availability as a source of comfort and help to suffering people is their answer to the question of theodicy. What suffering people need more than anything else is renewed strength to confront triumphantly the existential threat to their lives: not necessarily to obliterate evil totally, even though that clearly would be their desire, but, more important, to persevere in the confidence that, ultimately, victory over evil is guaranteed. That is the nature of their hope: unwavering confidence in the source of their victory, God.

Why the confidence? What is the ground of their hope? How do they know that God is on their side and not on the side of the evildoers? The answers to these questions constitute the substance of the inheritance that King received from his tradition, a tradition begun in the hidden meeting places where his enslaved ancestors encountered a divine friend with whom they talked and in whom they rejoiced. That experience constituted the nature of their faith or confidence and its corresponding implication, namely, loyalty and obedience. As surely as God had spoken to Moses and had revealed God's sensitivity to the suffering and pain of the Israelites, Africans in American slavery had had a similar experience with God. They had believed beyond a shadow of doubt that God would deliver them from their bondage and give them a life of blessedness. Similarly, they interpreted the life and ministry of Jesus of Nazareth, the incarnation of God in the world, not as that of a distant, powerful monarch but as that of a poor, marginalized, oppressed outcast who suffered thirst and hunger and homelessness and abuse and crucifixion at the hands of the nation's powerful religious and political leaders. Both before and during slavery, Africans in America had experienced God as an authentic friend, one who had accompanied them from Africa through the Middle Passage and had enabled them to survive. That was the evidence of God's true friendship, which, being divine, endures forever.

Thus, for African Americans, evil was not a metaphysical problem but a daily experience inflicted on human beings by human beings. In the biblical stories, African Americans had discovered a kind of duality between God's goodness toward humans on the one hand and human opposition to God on the other hand. The clearest examples of that duality are in the creation stories, which characterize the origin of the world as a state of perfect harmony complete with natural abundance and human flourishing. Similar portrayals appear in the eschatological visions of both the Hebrew and Christian Scriptures. In the creation stories, human beings are depicted as willfully disobeying God's command and, consequently, deliberately thwarting the divine purpose and causing their own fundamental fault or sin.

The stories clearly teach that activity undertaken in opposition to God's purpose inevitably results in moral disruption. In other words, by opposing the Creator's design, the creature misses the mark, and the cumulative effect of such continuous activities constitutes the nature of evil in the world. Thus, deeply rooted in the Genesis account of sin, the African American Christian tradition emphasizes an anthropological understanding of evil. Human beings participate in its cause and history is its locus. This Adamic myth corresponds with traditional African religious thought, which views God as infinitely good and incapable of initiating evil.

Thus, African Americans have always believed that human beings are a major causal factor of evil in the world, the paramount example of which is slavery. Conversely, they have believed also that the good in the world invariably results from humankind acting in concert with God's justice. Such activity implies partnership with God, because humankind cannot do it alone without excluding God from history and thereby deifying itself. That was the original mistake. Since God will not act as a divine monarch and destroy human freedom by imposing the good on the world, human beings and God must work together in order to preserve the true nature of both God and humankind. It is God's nature to struggle against evil in God's own way. Since the universe was created with moral structure and human beings were created in God's image, the partnership between them bestows dignity and freedom on human beings as they develop the capacity to discern evil and to resist it.

This necessary partnership with God in effecting justice in the world enabled King to level strong criticisms against humanists who relied on human efforts alone to achieve justice and peace. Similarly, he castigated those who waited on God alone to restore the brokenness of creation and who believed there was nothing that humankind could do that would have ultimate meaning. The former attitude he associated with the Renaissance view of humanity, the latter with the Reformation view; the former being overly optimistic, the latter overly pessimistic.[10]

King synthesized the two positions into a third position, thus including the limited perspectives of each. Humankind must cooperate with God in eradicating evil from the world. And cooperation will lead inevitably to the final victory. The theme song of the civil rights movement expressed that message in the clearest possible way.

> We shall overcome,
> We shall overcome,
> We shall overcome, someday.
> Oh, deep in my heart,
> I do believe,
> We shall overcome someday.

## THE TRUSTWORTHINESS OF GOD

As humankind's divine friend, Africans in America discovered, God was reliable in God's faithfulness because God was God and, unlike humans, God did not contradict God's self. As divine friend, God could be relied upon to work God's power because God not only created the universe and all therein but maintains and preserves it from the beginning until the end of time. As divine friend, God could be relied upon to act with justice because of God's liberating activity in the experience of the Hebrews, as depicted in the exodus; in the teaching of the prophets; in the life and teaching of Jesus of Nazareth. As divine friend, God could be relied upon to show love because, even while dying on the cross, Jesus, the incarnate God, exemplified divine forgiveness by praying for the forgiveness of his killers. Such an act demonstrated more clearly than any other his unceasing quest for the restoration of broken community. From the perspective of enslaved Africans, their suffering at the hands of evil was ennobled by the similar suffering of Jesus. Yet, let us hasten to state, neither African Americans nor Jesus ever romanticized suffering. It is evil inflicted on God's creation for the sake of destruction. Resistance to evil through the instrumentality of love is the message of the gospel. All who undertake such resistance, however, must inevitably suffer because they do battle against evil, which is a powerful oppositional force. Such suffering King called *redemptive*.

Trust in God constituted the source of King's hope and that of the people who followed him. In this faith and this hope we see the first principle of effectiveness in mobilizing his followers. This faith and this hope had been long established and regularly celebrated in the African American Christian tradition. Thus, they sang in slavery what they sang in the 1960s and even sing today:

> Didn't my Lord deliver Daniel,
> Deliver Daniel, deliver Daniel?
> Didn't my Lord deliver Daniel,
> An' why not a [sic] every man?

> He delivered Daniel from the lion's den,
> Jonah from de belly of de whale,
> And the Hebrew chillun from de fiery furnace,
> And why not every man?

The question in this song, "Why not every man?" is not raised for the purpose of expressing doubt but as a declaration of faith. That which God did for Daniel and Jonah and the Hebrew children evidences what God will do for all people. But God does not do it apart from human action, which is set in motion by desires and deliberate decisions.

The necessity of desire is extremely important, because it alone sets human action in motion. In the absence of desire there can be no action. Love, justice, and power will move nothing apart from the impetus of desire. Desire is the first principle of action. Hence, psychology is our starting point, and the evaluation of the quality of desire is what we might call moral psychology, which is a constitutive part of ethics. Thus, King spoke often of the so-called New Negro who had emerged in the movement: a person no longer willing to be merely passive in the face of evil but one who had become emboldened by the activity of resisting evil in the service of expanding and enhancing moral community.

## CHRISTIAN HOPE

To hope is to desire that which is possible of realization. As desire can be weak or strong, good or bad, so also hope can vary both in intensity and in quality. Our hope can be either confident or weak. Christian hope in the eschatological vision of God's sovereign rule is often focused on that which God as God will do. The moral implications of Christian hope have not been well developed, even though some of the groundwork for such has been laid by some of the theologians of hope, spearheaded by Jürgen Moltmann and others.

Unfortunately, the "otherworldly" dimension of Christian hope has led some to personalize so-called salvation history and sacrifice social and political involvement in favor of personal salvation *sola*. King's theology argues the reverse, namely, that the eschatological hope provides the foundational dynamic for social and political change because of its teleological status. That is to say, all historical matters are viewed as means to that final end. Thus, in lyrical prose, King eloquently set forth his belief in the triumphal power of love in his acceptance speech of the Nobel Peace Prize.[11]

In King's endeavor to console the family and friends of the children who had been martyred in the Sixteenth Street Baptist Church in Birmingham, he expressed the hope that they could find some consolation from the Christian affirmation that death is not the end but an open door to eternal life for those who die in the faith. It was significant for him that the children had died in church reflecting on the meaning of eternal truths. Further, he felt confident that their deaths might well lead the South to transform its negative history into a positive future.

## LOVE, POWER, AND JUSTICE

Building on the moral foundation of the Christian hope that King internalized from the black Christian tradition, his theological ethic was based on the principles of love, justice, and power, which were also rooted in his doctrine of God. King frequently acknowledged his indebtedness to various theologians who had influenced him immensely in his endeavor to make his faith intellectually credible. Yet none influenced him more than Paul Tillich in his understanding of the relation of these three ethical principles, love, power, and justice. Nowhere is Tillich's influence so clearly seen as in King's discussion of these principles in his final book, in which he engages in debate with the advocates of black power.[12] Tillich's analysis of power and its integral relationship with love and justice made an indelible impression on King for at least two reasons: (1) few, if any, Protestant theologians had a positive theology of power; and (2) none had demonstrated the harmonious relationship of love, justice, and power in God and the implications of that unity for Christian action in the world. Admittedly, Tillich's analysis relies on philosophical and theological methodologies, the unity of which he called a method of correlation. Accordingly, love, defined as the reunion of the separated, is represented biblically by the theological symbol Christ the Redeemer; power, defined as the capacity of being to pursue purpose, is represented theologically by the symbol God the Creator; justice, defined as the form that the reunion takes in legal and judicial structures, is represented biblically by the symbol God the Judge.

King's Tillichian understanding of love as an ontological principle and its correlation with the biblical view of love as *agapê* enabled him to see clearly that this type of love is different from sentiment. That is, our love for people is rooted not in warm feelings for them but in the necessity of reconciling those who are estranged for the sake of God's purpose for the world. When viewed as the reunion of the separated, love not only reflects the reconciling disposition of African Americans toward their white oppressors but also functions as an analytical principle. Thus, King was able to discern that those who habitually practice love become a loving people who cooperate with the divine power guiding the universe, while those who do not cooperate with that power become a hateful people. In light of the fact that we become what we do, King challenged his followers not to assume the character of their oppressors, and in turn, he challenged oppressors to cease their self-destructive activities.

Since hate cripples and destroys the doer as well as the victim, those who love not only preserve their own moral and spiritual integrity but also demonstrate to their oppressors the self-destructive nature of their hatred. Further, since love is at the heart of the cosmos, opposition to love implies hostility toward the whole of creation. Hence, King repeatedly contended that the struggle for civil rights was the struggle not for the redemption of black America alone but for the soul of all of America. Consequently, the goal King sought should never be viewed as merely utilitarian or pragmatic. Rather, his mission was a redemptive venture for all concerned: African Americans, the nation, and the world at large. As such, it was simultaneously theological, moral, and political. In brief, the goal was to create, expand, and preserve what he called "the beloved community" and the method of attaining it that he called "soul-force": the power of the spirit to resist every type of human abuse and to struggle for the conditions that would enable all humans to flourish.

King's conviction that love is the most durable power in the world inspired him to preach a sermon titled "The Most Durable Power."[13] In fact, he argued that love is the true answer to all human strivings over the centuries for the *summum bonum* of life. Most important, his understanding of love bore no hint of romanticism. Rather, he was fully aware that love always involves a willingness to sacrifice, and he kept that fact in the foreground of his teaching. He called this willingness to suffer by many names: "creative suffering," "redemptive suffering," "unmerited suffering."[14] Clearly, love was King's dominant ethical, theological, and political principle, permeating all his thought and practice. In his mind, the principle of love was implied whenever he spoke about nonviolent resistance, justice, peace, "brotherhood," community, reconciliation, freedom. All were derivative from his doctrine of God.

It is important to note that in King's understanding, God supports those who oppose evil only when they act in love and for the sake of the restoration of community. Strength and courage come from their faith in God's being with them, and that faith is the sign of God's grace. The agents become new people in their fight for a righteous cause. Praxis has a reflexive effect. Engagement in a cause shapes and reshapes character.

Further, we dare not ignore the fact that King viewed God's grace primarily as the source of inner strength and stability, and hence a source for psychological well-being. The source of King's courage was the confidence that God is able to give us inner peace in the midst of the trials and burdens of life. He believed that such inner stability was Jesus' main legacy to his disciples then and now. God offers neither material resources nor a magical formula that exempts us from suffering and persecution. Rather, God gives the gift of inner peace.

God and God's kingdom of love are at the heart of our universe as source and end. The Christian must be loyal to that center and strive to promote values that conform to that divine center. Hence, those who believe in God's sovereignty over the world should act against all who seek to establish a world based on principles that are contrary to God's rule. This is Christian moral action—acting to realize God's will with the awareness that such action must take precedence over social conformity and respectability. In other words, all such action must be prepared to risk everything and not count the cost. In that respect, the church should be the moral conscience of the nation and of the world. Gayraud Wilmore issues his strongest condemnation against the Euro-American churches in general and the Presbyterian Church in particular for their longtime collective refusal to bring their moral practices into compliance with their theological teachings concerning racial justice.

King was prone to speak of justice as the means that love takes in constituting genuine community, which was for him the final goal of the movement. He viewed community as the state of true neighborliness, where individuals willingly desire to be united as brothers and sisters, mutually supporting one another in all things. Wherever true community exists, one need not be concerned about justice, because all of the members will desire the well-being of one another. In other words, justice becomes an inner law written on the hearts of the people, rather than an external law that they inevitably will experience as an alien force. In this respect, he viewed the laws of desegregation as representative of external law, and that is why many experience them as alien when they are forced to obey them. Thus, for King, the goal of racial integration is synonymous with true neighborliness, when justice is inner law, written on the hearts of the people, and hence wholly desired.

Under the influence of Tillich's thought and the teaching of the African American Christian tradition, King never discussed power apart from its integral relation to love and justice. From the beginning, the power of the movement was spoken of as soul-force: the spiritual capacity to take a courageous stand for what is good and just, and to do so without counting the cost. In the face of terror, the use of soul-force is prior to the demands for any kind of power, because the separation of power from love and justice can lead only to varying forms of domination, as evidenced both at home and abroad.

Thus, I conclude (1) that King's theology and ethics are illustrative of the African American Christian tradition; (2) that theology and ethics are inextricably united; (3) that in the realm of race relations, the theology of the Presbyterian Church (U.S.A.) has been abstracted from the moral practices of social transformation; and (4) that the African American tradition within the Presbyterian Church represents a fitting corrective to the theological deficiency that Gayraud Wilmore addressed over two decades ago.

# Chapter 3

# Reformed Theology and Modern Culture
*Jan Rohls*

At the beginning of the twentieth century, German scholars discovered Reformed theology as one of the roots of modern culture. In his famous essay "The Protestant Ethic and the Spirit of Capitalism," the sociologist Max Weber, a Lutheran by birth, drew a connection between the ethic of Calvinism, based on the doctrine of predestination, and the rational spirit of modern capitalism. Weber was supported by Ernst Troeltsch, at that time his colleague in the Faculty of Divinity at Heidelberg University. Weber's essay was published in 1905, and Troeltsch's long article on Protestant Christianity and church in modern times appeared the next year. Troeltsch summarized his argument five years later in his famous essay on the relevance of Protestantism for the rise of the modern world. Troeltsch, also a Lutheran, compared the different branches of Protestantism and came to the conclusion that Calvinism was much more influential on modern society than Lutheranism.

Before discussing this thesis, let us remember the context in which all these arguments were formulated. In the late nineteenth and early twentieth centuries, the newly founded German Empire was trying to find its place among the nations. Despite the fact that it had a large Catholic population, its Prussian heritage made it a state dominated by Protestantism. The conflict between the liberals and the Catholic Church stood at the foundation of the empire. So, when Weber and Troeltsch were writing about the influence of Protestantism on certain aspects of modern culture and society, they were thinking in terms of the superiority of Protestantism over Roman Catholicism. For them, Catholicism belonged to the Middle Ages, and the triumph of neo-Thomism at the end of the First Vatican Council was proof of this conviction. It was neo-Thomism that also dominated the social doctrine of the Roman Church as expressed in the encyclical *Rerum novarum*, launched by Pope Leo XIII in 1891. Thus, Weber and Troeltsch were convinced that, among the Christian confessions, it was Protestantism, and not Catholicism, that took the side of modernity. Catholicism was regarded as traditional and linked with rural populations, while Protestantism was described as progressive and connected with industrial society.

However, that Weber and Troeltsch attributed general superiority to Protestantism does not explain why they were convinced of a special relationship between Calvinism and modern culture. Here, too, one must take into account the historical situation in which they formulated their theses. At this time, the young German Empire was comparing its own culture with the cultures of the dominant nations of Western Europe, such as France and Great Britain, and the rising power of the United States. As far as France is concerned, one was horrified by the antireligious aspects of the French Revolution and its consequences. In this respect Britain and North America showed a quite different development. There, the birth of modern society was closely linked with Protestant religion. In contrast to the German situation, however, where only a minority of the Protestant population belonged to the Reformed church, in England, Scotland, and the North American colonies, Calvinism, in its different forms, was the leading confession. Together with the Republic of the Netherlands, which at an early stage was also dominated by the Reformed church, these Western countries had something in common: politically and economically, they were regarded as the leading powers of modernity. The trade of the Dutch Republic, the industrial revolution in Britain, and American democracy formed a picture of a modern civilization that was somewhat different from German culture.

Should one inquire as to the reasons for this difference, the initial impression may be that the differences of confession played a central role. Among the Protestant denominations, Lutheranism was regarded as more traditional, whereas Calvinism was considered the progressive force that drove Dutch, British, and American society. Weber and Troeltsch found this thesis in the famous Stone Lectures delivered by the Dutch prime minister and theologian Abraham Kuyper at Princeton in 1899. In these lectures, Kuyper addressed the relationships between Calvinism, history, religion, politics, science, the arts, and the future. I consider here whether the conclusions Kuyper drew are correct or whether one must reexamine the relationship he found between Reformed theology and modern culture.

## REFORMED THEOLOGY AND CAPITALISM

Let us start with the relationship between Reformed Protestantism and capitalism. Max Weber regarded capitalism specifically as a modern phenomenon. It presupposes a certain mentality, namely, the goal of enlarging capital. The acquisition of money is no longer seen as an instrument to satisfy certain material needs but as an end in itself. To explain this capitalistic mentality, it is not sufficient to point to Luther's new conception of occupation as calling or vocation, for Luther regarded the vocation as a dispensation of God's providence that has to be accepted by humans. His high valuation of worldly occupations was a result of his criticism of monastic life, but it does not explain the specific activity connected with capitalism. Rather, capitalism presupposes a very ascetic way of life, which Weber found in Calvinism. For him, it was a consequence of the central doctrine of Calvinism, predestination, that the world became totally secular. There was no longer anything in the world, neither priests nor sacraments nor church, that could function as mediator between man and God, for, from eternity, who is elected and who is condemned is determined by the will of God. Now the individual himself had to prove that he was elected, and had to prove it by the fruits of faith, that is, by moral activity. Everything the individual did had to be done for the glory of God. What had been earned by labor had not been earned for consumption but for investment. Capital was not to be spent but rather to be invested in new projects. Just here lies the connection between the ascetic way of life preached by Calvinist ministers and the spirit of rising capitalism. The capitalist middle class had only to strip away the religious connotations of Calvinist ethics to reach its goal. Thus the Calvinist mentality changed into the mentality of the capitalist middle class. Of course, there is a difference. Whereas the old Calvinist wanted to be a subject morally active in society, the modern individual in Western society has to be active in a quite different way. The modern individual has to do his job.

Now, is Weber's contention about the relationship between Calvinism and capitalism true? Did the Calvinist or Puritanical spirit shape modern capitalistic mentality in the way Weber suggested? One first of all has to take into account the fact that capitalism was not invented by the Reformation but dates back to the late Middle Ages. At the time of the Reformation, the most highly developed parts of Europe were the centers of commerce in northern Italy and Flanders. The attitude of the Reformers toward economy differed, depending on where they lived. Someone like Luther, teaching at Wittenberg and thus living in a region dominated by agriculture, thought of the economy in quite different terms from Calvin in Geneva, which, like Lyon, was an old city built on commerce. Despite the fact that the medieval church generally condemned usury, it had always made exceptions in certain cases. Thus, two centuries before Calvin entered the stage, the lord bishop of Geneva had granted the city the freedom to practice usury and established municipal laws regulating the interest rate. This freedom, which was substantial for a merchant town such as Geneva, was defended by Calvin, thereby sweeping away the arguments against usury taken from the Bible. He argued that the text from Luke, "If you lend to those from whom you hope to receive, what credit is that to you?" (Luke 6:34), had been misunderstood when it was applied to usury. What Jesus demands is that his people should help the poor without expecting any recompense. The text does not refer to lending at all but to charity. Those parts of the Old Testament that forbid usury between brothers in Israel (Deut. 23:19–21) were concerned only with a Jewish practice that no longer applied to Christians. Thus, usury was not forbidden by the Bible, and it was acceptable, except when it ran counter to equity and fraternal bonds. In the exposition of the Eighth Commandment in his commentary on the last four books of Moses, Calvin asks: "If someone rich and well-to-do, wishing to buy a good farm, borrows part of the sum he needs from his neighbor, why should not the lender derive some profit by way of income until the loan has been repaid? Many such cases arise daily in which, so far as equity is concerned, usury is no worse than a purchase."[1]

If we turn to look at those places in Europe where economic life flourished after the Reformation, we cannot detect any direct connection between Calvinism and the spirit of capitalism. It is quite true that the northern provinces of the Low Countries, which opposed Spain, soon became the leading economic power in Western Europe, Amsterdam becoming the new center of trade and banking. However, this rarely had anything to do with Calvinism as such. Weber's famous thesis linked the spirit of capitalism with the Calvinist doctrine of predestination. It is quite true that Calvin himself, as well as Theodore Beza and his followers, thought that from the time of creation, each person was either elected or condemned. Moreover, they held that there are certain signs, such as faith or a holy life, by which the believer can detect whether he or she belongs to the elect. The term used to express this is the so-called practical syllogism. There is, however, no connection between this Calvinist doctrine of predestination and the spirit of capitalism. It is no wonder, then, that as proof of his thesis Weber quoted documents that do not belong to the real Calvinist tradition.

If we take a look at the Dutch Republic again, it becomes clear very quickly that it was not Calvinist ethics that formed the mind of the tradesmen, ship owners, and bankers in Amsterdam. Instead, it was the liberal climate of the republic that allowed economy to flourish. We must not think that the members of such great companies as the East India Company were all adherents of the Synod of Dort, where the strong Calvinist version of the doctrine of predestination triumphed. It is much more probable to find them in the Arminian camp, where free will played a larger role than in orthodox Calvinism. One finds also nothing in the Calvinist textbooks of ethics to support Weber's thesis that there is a connection between Calvinist ethics and the spirit of capitalism. The main characteristic of capitalism is the self-interest of the employer, whereas Calvinist ethics never regarded enrichment as such as the aim of economic activity. One worked to meet one's needs and to help the poor. Thus, earning money was always linked with charity as a Christian virtue. No wonder the Calvinist ministers so often had to warn the members of the great companies not to forget their main task in sending ships to East or West India: namely, to convert the natives and make them good Calvinists.

Let me restate my thesis: It was not the spirit of Calvinism that supported the development of capitalism in the Dutch Republic but the spirit of liberalism. One must always take into account that the republic was not a Calvinist country. The Calvinist church was the main church, but it never ruled the state. In this respect the Dutch Republic resembled the Republic of Venice, which was Catholic but resisted the institutions and spirit of the Counter-Reformation. It was in just this liberal climate of the Dutch Republic that trade and banking flourished. In a way, both the Dutch and the Venetian republics were old-fashioned in this respect. They defended the liberty of the medieval urban republics against the clericalization of the state. By contrast, in places such as Italy and Flanders, where economy had flourished before, it was set back by the Spanish Counter-Reformation.

It is quite true that a capitalist economy requires a special mentality. But activity and self-control, which Weber saw as a special mark of Calvinism, were general signs of the time. They were the consequence not of the Calvinist doctrine of predestination but of a tendency dating back to the late Middle Ages. The emphasis on sanctification and the importance of church censures in Calvinism clearly supported this tendency. The same holds true of neo-Stoicism, however, which was the most fashionable ethics of that time; here one could find the same interest in controlling the affections and passions. Additionally, neo-Stoicism was not restricted to any confession of the post-Reformation era. Since the late Middle Ages one could see everywhere in Europe how such virtues as frugality, economy, and industry were becoming more and more important. Begging, quite common before, was forbidden, and beggars were put into workhouses. All this had to do with the formation of early modern society and state; it was not restricted to Calvinism but can also be found in Catholicism. So let me say it again: The spirit of capitalism has no special affinity with Calvinist ethics. It makes no sense to say that it was Calvinist ethics that made the triumph of capitalism in modern culture possible.

## REFORMED THEOLOGY AND DEMOCRACY

At the same time that Weber formulated his thesis that Calvinism and capitalism belong together, Troeltsch drew a connection between Calvinism and democracy. At first glance, this thesis is as attractive as the first one. Like Weber in his thesis about capitalism, Troeltsch focused on the Anglo-American world when he thought of the affinity between Calvinism and democracy. He did not claim that Calvin himself was a defender of democracy, and even the structure of the church in Geneva was by no means democratic. The link between the church and the republic, however, nevertheless implied certain democratic tendencies, which fully emerged when Beza and the French Calvinists opposed the politics of the Parisian court. Troeltsch discussed at length the monarchomachic literature: Beza's *De jure magistratuum*, François Hotman's *Franco-Gallia*, and Philippe Duplessis-Mornay's *Vindiciae contra tyrannos*. The central ideas expressed in these works—the sovereignty of the people, the contract between the people and the king, and the right of resistance—Troeltsch regarded as the established doctrine of the school of Geneva. Even though these ideas are not essentially democratic, Troeltsch was convinced that Calvinism had inherent tendencies that made it easy to combine with democracy. Thus, he tried to trace back the Anglo-American alliance of Calvinism with democracy, finding its roots in Calvin's Geneva. His thesis amounts to this: despite the fact that democracy was developed neither by Calvin nor by his followers in the sixteenth and seventeenth centuries, Calvinism nevertheless has a certain affinity with democracy. This was also maintained by Kuyper in a much stronger sense, for he saw Calvinism as the off-spring of constitutional freedom. It is quite interesting to see how a left-wing Reformed theologian such as Jürgen Moltmann, who opposes Weber's thesis of a close affinity between Calvinism and capitalism, readily accepts the claim that Calvinism is closely related to democracy.

As in the case of capitalism, I doubt there is any special affinity between Calvinism and democracy. First of all, one has to admit that there is a striking difference between Zwingli and Calvin, Zurich and Geneva, as far as the relationship between church and state is concerned. What Zwingli established at Zurich was a state church in the strict sense. The church was not governed by an independent institution but by the council of the state. This was a solution that, in many respects, resembled the situation in Lutheran territories and in the Church of England, and it was later strongly defended by Thomas Erastus. In Geneva, however, we find a quite different solution; for Calvin, inspired by Martin Bucer in Strasbourg, was convinced that the church had to be a body governed by itself. Despite the fact that for Calvin, as for Zwingli, the relationship between church and state was a very close one, he nevertheless insisted on the independence of the church. This found its expression in the consistory, which governed the church and was responsible for church censures, whereas in Zurich there was no independent jurisdiction of the church. It was the question of church censures that led Calvin to his idea that there should be a church jurisdiction independent from the jurisdiction of the council. Thus he needed an independent body to be responsible for it. But this sort of church government was by no means democratic, as Kuyper assumed when he remarked that, because of the sovereignty of God and the monarchy of Christ, the earthly government of the church had to be democratic. Even when we go further and look at the structure of the church in those territories where different Reformed parishes formed one church, as in France and the Netherlands, it was not democratic at all. It is true that in this case the consistories sent their delegates to the provincial or national synods, but since the elders of the consistories were not elected directly by the members of the local church, neither the consistories nor the synods were democratic institutions. In fact, the attempt of Duplessis-Mornay to introduce elections of the ministers and elders by the congregation was rejected by the French national synod. Like the councils of the cities, the government of the Calvinist church was much more aristocratic than democratic; the elders were not elected by the congregation but rather co-opted by the members of the consistory. Therefore, one cannot say that the structure of the Calvinist church had any affinity with democracy.

Let us now turn to the relationship between church and state; perhaps here there are democratic tendencies within Calvinism. I concentrate on the development of Calvinist political thought in France, for in this case it becomes quite clear that there is no necessary affinity between Calvinism and democracy. As far as Calvin himself is concerned, he shared the common opinion of the Reformers that one had to obey the ruling authority, either the king or the magistrate. In cases where there was a conflict between the will of God and the will of the king, however, he conceded not only civil disobedience but also intervention from the princes of the blood, the Estates-General, and the inferior magistrates. Thus the inferior magistrates had the right to oppose tyranny, and they are compared to the ephors in ancient Sparta, who likewise controlled the kings. The subject of resistance became relevant when the Huguenots in France planned the conspiracy of Amboise to stop the influence of the Guises on the young king. While Calvin himself condemned the conspiracy, it was supported by his colleague Beza.

Between the conspiracy of Amboise of 1560 and the massacre of Saint Bartholomew of 1572, a large number of works concerning the right of resistance were produced. In 1573 the *Franco-Gallia* of François Hotman was published, followed by Beza's pamphlet *Du droit des magistrats sur leurs sujets* one year later and the *Vindiciae contra tyrannos* of Philippe Duplessis-Mornay in 1579. In these monarchomachic writings, the royal authority was limited by the power of the Estates, who supervised the king and could eventually depose him. The Estates-General thereby represented the people and had the power to act in the name of the people. In the Estates-General the inferior magistrates could express their opinions and thus played a controlling role quite similar to that of the ephors of ancient Sparta of which Calvin was speaking. For the monarchomachists, the state was based on a mutual contract between the people and the king. When the king broke the contract and became a tyrant, the people, represented by the inferior magistrates, had the right to resist. Thus, the contract between the people and the monarch was in fact a contract between the inferior magistrates and the king. However, this contract was rooted in an even higher contract between God and the king, by which the king was obliged to govern in the name of God: that is, with justice. The magistrates, then, had to determine whether the king fulfilled the duty resulting from the contract with God. Indeed, here as later in the *Politica* of John Althusius, we see a political theory in which monarchy and sovereignty of the people are combined by the thought that the monarchy consists of two contracts: a contract between God and the king and a contract between the king and the magistrates, who acted as representatives of the people.

This monarchomachic theory has been characterized as regarding its regime as formally monarchical, its basis as democratic, and its government as aristocratic. Royal authority was still conferred by God, but it was controlled by the people as represented by the magistrates. There was a democratic element in it, but on the whole the monarchomachic theory posulated a limited monarchy. Thus, from the political ideas of the monarchomachs, one cannot draw the conclusion that Calvinism had a strong affinity with democracy. If one looks for the origins of these ideas, one finds them in the scholastic theory of resistance and popular sovereignty. Marsilius of Padua, as well as Occam and Pierre d'Ailly, shared the idea that the power of the king is restricted and bound to the sovereignty of the people. Further, one has to take into account that much of what Beza and his fellow monarchomachians said was put forward some years earlier by the Lutherans of Magdeburg, which was the center of Protestant resistance against the emperor. This makes it even more improbable that there is a special affinity of Calvinism with democracy whereas Lutheranism prefers an authoritarian political structure.

The conviction of a relation between Calvinism and democracy is even more shaken if we look at the later development of Calvinist political thought in France. For even Duplessis-Mornay changed his political view and began to look for a strong king who would be able to guarantee toleration of the Huguenots. When Henry of Navarre, a Calvinist, became king of France, the Huguenots accepted absolutist ideas as developed by the party of the Politiques. Michel Hurault, the Calvinist grandson of the chancellor Michel de l'Hôpital, the head of this party, defended absolutism in his *Excellent et libre discours sur l'estat présent de la France*, published in 1588, as the only possibility to pacify France. After the Edict of Nantes, the Huguenots became strong supporters of the absolutism established by the former Calvinist, Henry IV. For them, only a strong king was able to guarantee the religious tolerance of the edict. It was not the absolute king they feared but the Catholic clergy, especially the Jesuits. Absolutism was regarded as an advance over the anarchy of the Wars of Religion. For this reason, the famous Calvinist academies of Saumur and Sedan taught absolutism as the favored political theory, as, for example, in Moise Amyraut's *Discours sur la souverainité des rois* of 1650. The French monarch in his kingdom was regarded as the true image of God who presides over the world. Like God, he has no superior nor equal, for he concentrates in his person all the majesty of the state.

The defense of absolutism by the French Calvinists went so far that they also heavily criticized the English Revolution. Far from revealing any true revolutionary spirit of the Reformed religion, the Independents of the revolution separated themselves from true orthodox Calvinism. They no longer regarded synods as essential but insisted on the independence of the local parish. Even after the revocation of the Edict of Nantes, intellectuals of the Refuge still defended absolutism. In his *Avis aux réfugiés*, Pierre Bayle heavily attacked those Calvinists who sympathized with the Glorious Revolution. In his view, absolutism was the best form of government, since it alone was able to save people from anarchy. Of course, this did not mean that Bayle also supported the anti-Calvinist politics of Louis XIV. On the contrary, he thought that it would be much wiser to tolerate religious minorities such as the Huguenots in France in order to transform them into loyal subjects. His plea for religious tolerance thus had nothing to do with antiabsolutism. Instead it was his antagonist, the orthodox Calvinist Pierre Jurieu, who combined religious intolerance with a critique of absolutism. Because he still dreamed of a final victory of Calvinism in France, he defended the idea of an invasion by the future king of England, William of Orange.

In general, one can say that after the revocation of the Edict of Nantes, the Huguenot emigrants adopted the political thought of the countries where they settled. Even then, after all they had experienced, the French Calvinists were not drawn to the idea of democracy. In the Netherlands they supported the relatively liberal society, in England the constitutional monarchy of William of Orange, and in Prussia the absolutism of the elector. Thus, in 1707, Armand Dubourdieu, son of a French emigrant and minister at the church of the Savoy in London, could declare: "There are among us those who subscribe to the thesis of the power of kings; such extreme ideas have undermined our churches. Thanks to God I did not study my theology concerning the power of kings in the works of Amyraut and Merlat, nor in the *Avis aux réfugiés*. I have been nurtured since my childhood on the principles of liberty in a free country. I am French by birth, but in this respect I have an English heart."[2]

## REFORMED THEOLOGY, ARTS, AND SCIENCE

When Kuyper held his lectures on Calvinism, European aestheticism had reached its peak. It was a reaction against the rule of science and technology. The arts were regarded as a medicine to cure people from the materialism closely linked to the natural sciences. In this situation Kuyper defended Calvinism against the prejudice that it is an enemy of the arts. For him, the reason why Calvinism did not develop an aesthetic of its own lies in its nature; it does not regard the arts as an adequate medium for religion. Out of its unique elements, Calvinism was unable to create a new artistic style comparable to Baroque, which was the style that developed out of the Catholic Counter-Reformation. Kuyper even quoted Hegel, who taught that only in religions of a lower type, such as Greek polytheism, were the arts—sculpture, painting, music, and drama—regarded as an adequate medium for religious thought. If it is true, however, that Calvinism, being a higher form of religion, could not in principle generate a new artistic style, then what was its relation to the arts? Kuyper emphasized that Calvin himself thought of the arts as a gift from God. In addition, it was a great artistic achievement of Calvinism that the arts were liberated. They became independent from the church because the Reformed religion was totally spiritual. The Dutch painting of the golden age, the seventeenth century, was taken as strong evidence that painting became popular under the influence of Calvinism. Kuyper even linked the fact that the Dutch painters made everyday life an artistic subject with the Calvinist doctrine of election, for God's grace was no longer restricted to saints and priests. Thus it was Calvinism that freed painters from working only for the church and allowed them to choose their subject matter freely rather than having it dictated by the church.

Is Kuyper's view of the relationship between Calvinism and the rise of Dutch painting in the seventeenth century true? First of all, one has to take into account that Reformed theology indeed had quite a different relationship to painting from that held by either Roman Catholics or Lutherans. The prohibition of pictures in the Second Commandment was interpreted in a strict way. No paintings were allowed in the church. When the old buildings were taken over by the Calvinists, they removed the altarpieces as well as all other religious paintings. Calvin, like Zwingli, was not only convinced that religious paintings had no pedagogical value—a position not shared by Catholics and Lutherans—but even believed that having such paintings in church was contrary to the commandment of God. This created a special problem in the Netherlands; for here and in Italy Renaissance painting was born in the late Middle Ages. In the south, which remained Spanish and Catholic, painters such as Rubens and Van Dyk could still produce works for the church, but the case was quite different in the north. To be sure, not all of the population of the Dutch Republic was Calvinist, though Calvinism was the only officially acceptable confession. Compared to the south, however, the role of the Catholics was marginal, and the Anabaptist groups, like the Calvinists, had no interest in having paintings in their churches. Thus, on the whole, the church in the republic no longer supported painting; in the south the Catholic Church still employed painters for religious illustrations, but in the north the church ceased to be such an employer.

This did not mean that the production of paintings in the republic ceased. In fact, quite the opposite is true. There has never been such an increase in painting as in the Dutch Republic in the seventeenth century. Because it was no longer the church that now ordered paintings but the rich merchants and ship owners, as well as the different guilds and corporations, the growth of wealth in the young country spurred the increase in painting. Whereas before the church had ordered altarpieces, now the merchants ordered portraits; ship owners, maritime scenes; the guilds and corporations, group portraits. The discovery of everyday life that took place in Dutch painting of this period had nothing to do with any special Calvinist doctrine. Kuyper is wrong when he assumes that it was the doctrine of election through grace, with all its implications, that led to this development. The genre of paintings that show scenes from everyday life, as well as the still lifes, generally have a moral meaning that is not specifically Calvinist but rather reflects the neo-Stoic ethics that were very popular in the Dutch Republic at that time. Very often, the paintings are meant to remind us of the vanity of the world and of our own mortality. It is partially correct to say that the secularization of painting in the north of the Low Countries was influenced by Calvinism. It is true in that the altarpieces were banished from the church; but this does not mean that there was no longer any interest in religious painting. Quite the opposite is true. Instead of being commissioned for use in church, religious paintings such as those of Rembrandt were now ordered by private persons or secular institutions, and it was no longer the saints or legends that were pictured but scenes from the Bible.

It is therefore quite true that there is a connection between Reformed theology and painting in the Dutch Republic of the golden age. However, this connection is not the result of a direct influence of specific Calvinist doctrines on painting. Instead, the prohibition of altarpieces and religious paintings in the church, those items that were closely tied to worship, led to a secularization of Dutch painting in the described manner. A similar change occurred in the field of music. Organs, like altarpieces, were not allowed as parts of the purified religious worship because of the strict biblicism of Reformed theology. Since playing the organ during worship was forbidden, and the singing of psalms without instumental accompaniment became the only church music allowed in Reformed worship, the organ again became a secular instrument. Because the organs in the Netherlands, like the churches, belonged to the towns, the magistrates did not have them destroyed but rather used them for secular concerts. From this time on, one could find church concerts that had nothing at all to do with religious worship. Thus, painting and organ playing became secular in the sense that there was no connection to the Reformed worship service.

Having discussed the relationship of Reformed theology to the arts, let me now draw attention to science. In his chapter about Calvinism and science, Kuyper discussed the founding of the University of Leiden by William of Orange, the invention of the telescope and microscope, and the development of empirical science at this famous place. Kuyper was interested in showing how the development of science has its roots in Calvinism. He argued that the doctrine of predestination led to the conviction that nature is governed by laws that the scientist has only to discover. The Calvinist doctrine of predestination and the fundamental conviction of modern science thus have a common foundation. Both regard the world as grounded in a principle of determination. Calvinism, therefore, with its deterministic view of the creation, is much closer to modern science than Arminianism. However, Kuyper also thought that the doctrine of common grace, which he also found in Calvin's teaching, was as important to the development of modern science as the dogma of absolute predestination. Despite the fact that we are corrupted by sin, God does not destroy us and the world in which we live but preserves all by common grace. Reformed theology therefore emphasized that nature reveals God as creator and preserver of the world. Whereas the Middle Ages saw very little scientific research, the Calvinist doctrine of common grace inspired the rise of natural science in early modernity.

Let us now address Kuyper's thesis that Reformed theology made the most important contribution to modern natural science. Kuyper was by no means the only theologian who maintained an affinity between Calvinism and modern science. However, I think one can show that there is no real connection between specific Calvinist doctrines and the rise of modern science in the sixteenth and seventeenth centuries. It is quite true that Calvin himself regarded the natural world as a mirror that reflects God, even as the theater of God's glory in which we are placed as spectators. This does not mean, however, that he was in any way interested in scientific research per se. Additionally, he was convinced that some of the biblical descriptions of the creation were accommodated to the mentality of the simple-minded people of antiquity. Thus, in his commentary on Genesis, he declared that Moses does not usually speak in a scientific mode but rather in a popular one. Once again, this does not mean that Calvin himself in any way opened the way for modern cosmology; his cosmology was geocentric, not only because that was the accepted astronomical view of his day but also because it was supported by the Bible. Both Girolamo Zanchi and Lambertus Danaeus were deeply influenced by Calvin, and each wrote a Christian physics based on the Bible and Aristotle, in which the beginning of the Bible is interpreted quite literally. Thus Danaeus thinks that the world was really created in six days, and that the world does not move is proved by the usual quotations from the Bible. In these works, the heliocentric cosmology of Copernicus is not accepted; on the contrary, it is heavily attacked because it contradicts the Bible. It should be clear by now that there is no direct way from Calvin and his pupils to modern science. Even later, almost in the middle of the seventeenth century, Voetius, the famous head of Dutch Reformed orthodoxy, criticized those who no longer stuck to the Mosaic physics of Holy Scipture, which is dictated by the Holy Spirit, but instead trusted their own observations.

If we want to find out when Reformed theology started to accept modern science, we have to look at the influence of Descartes. It was the French philosopher who supported modern physics with its heliocentric cosmology, and it was in the Netherlands that Reformed theologians and philosophers first introduced Cartesianism into their teaching at the universities. Neither Calvin himself nor any of his orthodox pupils contributed anything to the rise of modern science, but Calvinist theologians and philosophers such as Johannes Clauberg and Christoph Wittich were the first to accept modern science and its cosmology as presented by Descartes. In 1653, Jacob du Bois, a Reformed minister in Leiden, published his *Dialogus theologico-astronomicus*, in which he defended the geocentric cosmology as the only one supported by the Bible. Wittich, at that time teaching at the University of Leiden, wrote a response criticizing the misuse of the Holy Scripture in physics. In this treatise, for the first time, he combined the theory of accommodation with a defense of the heliocentric cosmology as taught by Descartes. Where the geocentric cosmology is presupposed, the author of the Bible, the Holy Spirit, accommodates himself to the ancient readers. For us, living in a quite different context, this cosmology has no relevance any longer, even though it is presupposed by the Bible. Wittich defends his view by a hermeneutical principle: the intention of the Holy Spirit while inspiring the authors to write the Bible was not to teach physics and cosmology but to tell us what to do in order to gain heaven. This was the end of the Christian physics of Danaeus, Zanchi, Voetius, and many others.

The consequence was that the picture the Bible gave of the universe could now be criticized. At the end of the seventeenth century, Balthasar Bekker, a minister in Amsterdam, published his famous book *De Betoverde Weereld*, in which he regarded the biblical teachings about spirits and demons and their influence on human bodies as an accommodation and as contradicting the Cartesian dualism of mind and body, which does not allow for such an influence. But neither Wittich nor Bekker represents a majority of the Dutch Reformed theologians of that time. They were heavily attacked by the defenders of Calvinist orthodoxy. Peter of Mastricht still recommended the Christian physics of Danaeus, and Melchior Leydecker explicitly defended the condemnation of Galileo by the Catholic Church.

## REFORMED THEOLOGY, RELIGION, AND HISTORY

When Kuyper held his famous Stone Lectures on Calvinism, he began with some reflections about Calvinism, history, and religion. He started with a definition of Calvinism. In a scientific sense, Calvinism means a certain principle essentially connected with a certain way of life that is characteristic of Western Europe and North America. Calvinism is a specific form of religion that expresses itself in theology, church order, and social life. It implies a specific vision of the relationship between nature and grace, Christianity and the world, church and state, and art and science. It is an axiom that determines our relation to God, humankind, and the world. This axiom is the sovereignty of God. Whereas for Luther the starting point was the justification of the sinner, for Calvin it was God and predestination. The foundation of Lutheranism is anthropological, while that of Calvinism is theological. It was this theological axiom that Kuyper understood to be responsible for the affinity between Calvinism and modern culture. For example, because of the sovereignty of God we are all equal before God, and thus Calvinism in this sense has a strong affinity to democracy. Some years after Kuyper had held his Stone Lectures, Weber and Troeltsch discussed the relation between Calvinism and modern culture, and they, too, emphasized the importance of the doctrine of predestination. Both regarded predestination as the central dogma of Calvinism.

Weber and Troeltsch, like Kuyper, leaned heavily on the confessional typology of Alexander Schweizer in his *Die Glaubenslehre der evangelisch-reformirten Kirche*, published between 1844 and 1847. Schweizer was by no means a Reformed confessionalist but rather the most gifted pupil of Schleiermacher. But he was still concerned to show the relative right of the Reformed position within Protestantism alongside the rising Lutheran confessionalism. Both the Lutherans and the Reformed opposed Roman Catholicism, but they did so in different ways. Whereas the Lutherans attacked the Jewish aspects of Catholicism, the Reformed critique was directed against the pagan elements. While the Lutherans stressed faith against works, the Reformed stressed God against the world. Thus the Lutheran axiom was of an anthropological nature, the Reformed of a theological nature. The Reformed axiom was in fact identical with what Schleiermacher regarded as the essence of religion as such, the absolute dependence of man on God. As with Schleiermacher, however, this does not mean that we are totally passive; on the contrary, we are to glorify God with all our actions. Thus the religious feeling of absolute dependence, which found its dogmatic expression in the doctrine of predestination, is connected with continous moral activity. Even more than Lutheranism, it is Reformed Protestantism that Schleiermacher called the "teleological" form of piety.

In his comparative study on Lutheran and Reformed doctrine published in 1855, Matthias Schneckenburger claimed that the real difference between Lutherans and the Reformed is that the former are passive while the latter are active. Lutherans cling to justification by faith alone, while for the Reformed, sanctification and thus moral activity are of central importance. This understanding of the difference between Lutherans and Reformed became very influential. In his essays on church polity, Karl Bernhard Hundeshagen regarded passivity as a shortcoming of Lutheran Protestantism. Quietism was given as the reason why Lutheranism failed to build up a new society. Thus, since the middle of the nineteenth century, a twofold essence of Reformed Protestantism was postulated: the doctrine that humankind is totally dependent on God and the corresponding moral activity of human beings who, by their sanctification, glorify God. In this light, it becomes very easy to trace the connection between Reformed Protestantism and modern culture; it was restless moral activity that changed the Western world. Weber and Troeltsch merely drew the sociological consequences from the confessional typology developed by Schweizer, Schneckenburger, and Hundeshagen when they postulated a special relationship between Reformed theology and modern culture.

We should also question, however, whether the doctrine of absolute predestination is truly the central dogma of the Reformed church. Examining Calvin's *Institutio*, one can clearly see how the Augustinian doctrine of divine election as an expression of God's free grace became more and more important in subsequent editions. Similarly, Beza placed the doctrine of God's eternal decrees at the top of his *Summa totius Christianismi*. As a result, he defended supralapsarianism in its strongest form. Even though the Synod of Dort made no final declaration on the orthodoxy of infralapsarianism and supralapsarianism, the leading heads of the Dutch Calvinist orthodoxy were supralapsarians. Thus, at first glance, it seems quite reasonable to regard the doctrine of absolute predestination as the central dogma of the Reformed church. However, the strong defense of the doctrine at Dort and in the Formula Helvetica at the end of the seventeenth century showed that it was not supported by all Reformed theologians, either in the Dutch Republic or in other countries. Indeed, for theologians such as Caspar Olevian, Heinrich Bullinger, and later Johannes Cocceius, for whom the idea of the covenant between God and man was of paramount importance, the doctrine of predestination never played as crucial a role as it did for Beza. Moreover, it was within the Reformed church that Arminius heavily opposed this doctrine by defending free will. Finally, if we examine the confessions, we find that one of the most important confessions, the Heidelberg Catechism, does not even mention predestination. Especially in the German Reformed territories, predestination was never regarded as the central dogma. For this reason, the elector of Brandenburg, who at the beginning of the seventeenth century converted to Calvinism, did not send a deputy to the international Synod of Dort, where the doctrine of absolute predestination became a dogma of the Dutch church and where the Arminians were excluded.

Thus, the doctrine of predestination never played the central role ascribed to it by Schweizer and others. It is not by chance, however, that in the middle of the nineteenth century Schweizer regarded the doctrine of absolute predestination as the central dogma of the Reformed church. His teacher, Schleiermacher, had revived just this doctrine, which had been heavily criticized during the Enlightenment. Neither Schleiermacher nor Schweizer simply restored the old Calvinist dogma; rather, both changed it in a very important respect. Schleiermacher had defended Calvin's teaching on predestination against the Lutheran Karl Gottlieb Bretschneider. This was the result not so much of his own Reformed background as of the Spinozism reflected in his definition of piety or religion as a feeling of absolute dependence; for it is this absolute dependence that is also expressed in the doctrine of predestination. Now, both Schleiermacher and Schweizer rejected the old doctrine of double predestination; for them, predestination was absolute, but a predestination to salvation alone. The old dualistic view was thereby abandoned, and they taught instead a universal salvation of all. Despite their conviction that the old doctrine of predestination was the central dogma of Reformed Protestantism, they were equally sure that this dogma had been gravely criticized and had lost its central place. A return to it was not considered possible. Rather, leaving aside the dualism of election and reprobation, they completely transformed it.

Schleiermacher and Schweizer thus transformed the old dogma of predestination because they were convinced that there was no way back to it. This was not the opinion only of two Reformed theologians of the nineteenth century but also of their most eminent adversary of the twentieth century. Karl Barth, too, replaced the old dualistic version of predestination with one that implies the universality of God's grace. In all these cases, the supposed central dogma of the Reformed church was completely changed and became something quite different from what it was in the time of Calvin or Voetius. Like the Lutherans, the Reformed also took part in that great transformation which led from the old Protestantism to the new. It was through this transformation that Reformed theology was reconciled with modern culture: a transformation that is not yet completed but is an ongoing task. For either Reformed theology will be able to give answers to the problems posed by the changing modern culture, or modern culture will lose its interest in Reformed theology.

# Chapter 4

# The Living God: The Problem of Divine Personality in Reformed Theology

*Dawn DeVries*

> *[E]veryone must recognize it as an almost absolute necessity for the highest stage of piety to acquire the conception of a personal God. . . . Yet the profoundest of the church fathers have ever sought to purify the idea. Were the definite expressions they have used to clear away what is human and limited in the form of personality put together, it would be as easy to say that they denied personality to God as that they ascribed it to Him.*
> —Schleiermacher, *On Religion*

Is it right to think of God as a person? I remember very clearly the time in my life when this question became a pressing theological concern for me. At the age of sixteen, I was diagnosed with a usually terminal disease, and within the first six months there were several occasions on which I came very close to death. Although I was raised in a Christian home, I had had a conversion experience as a young child that had set the tone of my life up to that point. I understood my entire existence as one determined by a personal relationship to God through Christ that I experienced chiefly in the practices of prayer and Bible study. Searching the Scripture, listening to sermons, and fervently calling on my heavenly Father, I sought to understand everything that happened to me as something God was arranging for me for his own wise and loving purposes. Lying in my hospital room alone one night back then, I remember thinking, "My Dad can barely bring himself to visit me in the hospital because he is so upset that I'm going to die. I know he loves me and I can feel his wrenching grief. Yet my heavenly Father seems strangely indifferent to my suffering. I pray to him and receive neither healing nor sympathy and comfort. Just absence. So is God actually who I thought he was?[1] Is God a wise and loving person who takes an interest in my daily life? It seems hardly possible that all the more trivial things I used to tell him about could be of any consequence to him if now, while I'm in the fight of my life, he's simply not to be bothered. I've never known another person like that—usually when the chips are down your friends come through." That train of thought was the beginning of a crisis of faith for me. And although I did eventually get better, I could not let go of the questions that swirled through my mind that night. Indeed, further theological problems were raised for me by my parents' explanation for my miraculous cure. I had been the beneficiary of many prayers—probably tens of thousands—and God had heard and answered these prayers. But I knew that the young girl in the bed next to me, who had died, was also well loved by her parents and prayed for by many friends. Why did I get better? Why did she die? Was God susceptible to bribery? And if God had answered my family's prayers, why did he continue to hide from me?

This existential crisis in my adolescence set me on a course that is responsible in large part for my pursuit of a vocation in theology. I thought I had lost my faith in God. But really, I had only lost faith in a particular way of understanding God, a doctrine I might now call "uncritical anthropomorphism." I had learned the hard way that God is not a person like my own father.

I want to make a modest contribution to understanding the broad witness of the Reformed tradition on the notion of God as person. I cannot, of course, do this exhaustively within the confines of a single essay. But I do believe we can make a start at determining whether the Reformed tradition has specific and perennial concerns that bear on the appropriateness of assigning personhood to God. In section 1, I discuss the dominant tendency in Reformed theology in the first half of the twentieth century, illustrating the intensification of the concept of God as person in works by Karl Barth (1886–1968), John Oman (1860–1939), Emil Brunner (1889–1966), and H. H. Farmer (1892–1981). In section 2, I go back to Calvin and Reformed orthodoxy to consider the continuity or discontinuity of these twentieth-century works with the older tradition. In section 3, I discuss two nineteenth-century Reformed theologians, Friedrich Schleiermacher (1768–1834) and A. E. Biedermann (1819–1885), who articulated strong arguments that either severely limit or deny the personhood of God. In conclusion, I try to draw out distinctive emphases from all the theologians I've discussed and suggest ways in which these concerns might contribute to current and future discussions on the doctrine of God in the Reformed tradition.

## GOD AS PERSON IN TWENTIETH-CENTURY THEOLOGY

Karl Barth's essay "Faith in a Personal God" was prepared for a meeting of the Swiss Reformed Society of Preachers (Schweizerische reformierte Predigergesellschaft), delivered in Aargau on May 19, 1913. His argument in this piece will surprise those who know of Barth only as the vehement critic of Protestant liberalism, for in this early address he displays the colors of his own theological formation by the Lutheran mediating theologian Wilhelm Herrmann. "The question about the personal nature of God," Barth writes, "has to do with what makes for better or worse dogmatics, and anyone who regards it as superfluous has thought too little about the task of theology."[2] The question whether God is personal, however, all turns on what is meant by the term *person*. Barth argues that A. E. Biedermann's substitute for divine personhood, that is, *Geist-sein,* or "Being Spirit," lacks precisely what it is that the concept of personhood contains in addition—that is, individuality. And this is a fatal flaw, because in religious experience we know God not as an abstract principle—"Being Spirit" (Biedermann) or "moral world order" (Fichte) or "substance" (Spinoza)—but as an individual, a very particular "he" who thinks and wills.[3] Religious experience receives God as absolute and as person at the same time.[4] But the opposition between what Barth calls "the Exalted" (*das Erhabene*) and the personal within the concept of God cannot finally be reconciled.

The challenge is to find a way of positing both even if we cannot think them together.[5] The source for both sides of our understanding of God is pious experience—especially the life in God that Jesus has awakened in us.[6] Christian religious experience gives rise to both ways of thinking about God: God as person and God as the exalted one transcending personal limitations. And it is because of the unity and tension of these pious experiences of God that the two ways of expressing God's nature doctrinally arise. We are permitted to say both things about God on the basis of this experience, Barth states, but there is finally no suitable formula for synthesizing them.

By the time he returned to the doctrine of God in his *Church Dogmatics* several decades later, Barth's position on divine personhood had altered significantly. For one thing, he was no longer in any way tempted to argue from Christian religious experience to a concept of God. The first principle of the *Church Dogmatics* is the assertion that God speaks and that human beings can only listen and receive God's self-revelation in Jesus Christ.[7] Under the influence of Martin Buber's "I-Thou" philosophy, however, Barth also changed the emphasis in his language for God. While in the early essay he struggled to balance personal and suprapersonal aspects of God and assert both at once, now he argues that God presents himself in revelation as the Supreme Subject—not an It but a Thou. Insofar as humans have knowledge of God, this is because God as subject makes himself object and makes humans subjects in relation to himself. In a total reversal of his argument in the early essay, Barth asserts that the very concept of personhood can be known only from God's self-disclosure of what true personhood is.[8] We must not start with a human concept of person and seek to apply it to the divine being but rather learn from the Supreme Subject what it means to be a person: namely, one who loves in the way God loves. God therefore is "not the personified but the personifying person—the person on the basis of whose prior existence alone we can speak (hypothetically) of other persons different from Him"[9]

Completely rejecting his earlier argument on the logical difficulties presented by applying personal language to God, Barth states:

> [I]t is not the case that this application of the personal manner of speech to God means the recognition of a paradox in the nature of God that we cannot unravel, because on the one hand we must necessarily understand God as the impersonal absolute, but at the same time . . . we must also understand Him as person. . . . [W]e must notice that the paradox of the nature of God that we cannot unravel is not in any sense that of a logical tension between two concepts which we can perceive and control as such, as if we knew what "absolute" is on the one hand and "personality" on the other, as if the difficulty consisted in bringing both together, and as if God's reality were just the overcoming of this difficulty. No: the (to us) inexplicable paradox of the nature of God . . . is the paradox of the combination of His grace and our lost condition, not the paradox of the combination of two for us logically irreconcilable concepts.[10]

Barth blames the wrong turns taken in the history of the doctrine of God on the church's unwitting adoption of Stoic and Neoplatonic concepts of God. When theology begins properly, with God's own self-revelation, there is no problem with calling God a person, because that is just who God shows himself to be: the One who loves in freedom. I could, of course, say much more about Barth's doctrine of God, but we must leave him for now and consider briefly some other early twentieth-century arguments for divine personality.

John Oman may not be a well-known theologian to most of us. He was professor of theology and later principal of Westminster College, Cambridge—the theological college of the Presbyterian Church of England—from 1907 to 1935. He is probably best known for his Gifford Lectures, published in 1931 as *The Natural and the Supernatural*, and to many he is remembered also as the first English translator of Schleiermacher's *Speeches on Religion*. In his study *Grace and Personality*, published in 1917, Oman mounts an interesting argument for understanding God as person. He starts with an entirely different problem than does Barth. The issue for him is the perennial controversy about grace and free will that appears and reappears in the history of Western theology, beginning with Augustine and Pelagius but repeating itself in the battles between Calvinists and Arminians in the seventeenth century and between Romantics and rationalists in the eighteenth and nineteenth centuries. The fact that this debate has never been resolved and keeps recurring suggests that there is a truth enshrined in both sides. The Pelagians are right, Oman thinks, to insist that God takes the human being seriously as a "moral personality." But the Augustinians are right to insist that religion is characterized by our absolute dependence on God. To move beyond the impasse between these two ways of understanding the operation of grace, Oman suggests that we need to scrutinize the concept of God that both sides presuppose a priori: that is, God as an irresistible, omniscient, and omnipotent force. Rather than beginning with a preconceived notion of God, Oman argues that the concept of God should be inferred from reflection on experience—especially that most fundamental human experience of the search for one's true self and for autonomy.[11]

As the human person seeks autonomy, at first this seems to be a call to absolute independence, and autonomous action is characterized by self-determination, self-direction, and self-consciousness. To grow in freedom toward autonomous moral selfhood is to experience ourselves as free to form our own character, to choose our own projects, and to come to an awareness of what our actions mean. But this apparent independence is only half of the story. The more the person grows in moral freedom, the more she becomes aware that her freedom is not absolute. Self-determined actions always occur as responses to situations that are given. And our ability to act according to our values, if this is to mean something more than acting according to our personal preferences, implies that there are objective values outside ourselves. Further, reality as we encounter it is not our own creation but something that is wholly provided for us. When we take into account all the ways in which the givenness of reality hems us in, it leads us to an acknowledgment of our dependence. The search for personal autonomy, then, leads humans to an ever deeper sense of their need to accept this dependence, or, to put it differently, to accept reality. The more one accepts reality, however, the more she is lured toward authentic autonomy, and it is precisely the way reality calls or beckons us toward growth in authentic autonomy that points to God as person. We do not encounter reality as something that violently thwarts our freedom or irresistibly dominates us. Rather, in the quest for true personhood, we discover a person-like providence that nurtures and encourages our growth. God's grace, then, is a way of speaking about the personal relation of the world to us in which we attain our own emancipation through the challenge, comfort, and encouragement that lead to our development as moral persons.[12]

Oman's objections to an impersonal concept of God are chiefly moral. He writes:

> What reason in the world . . . can there be, why, if grace can work impersonally and even have a material vehicle, it should not be efficacious over the whole realm at least of human affairs? Why should it pass in purity only through certain priestly channels, while all other rivers of truth and goodness may be polluted? No reason can be given except God's arbitrary will; and a will that could easily correct by power, and simply will not, is not good.[13]

No, the fact that human virtue is won only through the long hard struggle to attain it, through error and failure, suggests not a God who is evil or powerless but a God who is infinitely patient, like a parent who waits for the child to grow into a sense of his own mission in life. God's relation to us must be personal, for otherwise our own experience of growth in personhood makes no sense.[14] In the Gospels, God is presented as just such a loving Father whose dealings with human beings are totally trustworthy. We are taught by Jesus to read God's fatherly care not only in a special, sacred realm but in the whole range of our experience in the world—even the difficult experience of the indifference of nature. God's gracious care, Oman argues, "embraces all secularities" so that even experiences of extreme hindrance are transformed "with the light of His love shining on them and turning all their shadow into radiance."[15] This piety based in a gracious relationship is best epitomized in the theology of the Lord's Prayer and the Beatitudes. We are raised above the appearance of evil and meaningless-ness to a confidence that the world belongs to God and is ultimately good, and from this position of trusting dependence on God, we can become truly respon-sible human beings. The conflict between freedom and dependence, then, is resolved. For now, however, we must leave Oman and consider another argument for thinking of God as person.

Emil Brunner, professor of theology at the University of Zurich from 1924 to 1952, is well known as the early companion of Barth in the dialectical the-ology and champion of his own brand of neo-orthodoxy after his decisive break with Barth on the legitimacy of natural theology. Although he had already pub-lished several theological works, his 1938 study *Wahrheit als Begegnung,* trans-lated into English as *The Divine-Human Encounter,* marked a turning point in Brunner's theological development. In Martin Buber's "I-Thou" philosophy, Brunner believed he had discovered the key for recovering what he called "the Biblical-Reformation" understanding of God. The argument Brunner presents is quite straightforward. Since Christian theology's sole source and norm is the Bible, the theologian must take seriously the personal way in which the divine-human encounter is presented there. God is not presented as he is in himself but only as the one who approaches human beings; similarly, the Bible gives no general concept of humanity, but only an account of humankind as com-ing from God.[16] They meet in the dynamic of an ongoing series of events in which God wills the free response of creatures in faith and love. God commu-nicates himself through the Word, and human beings respond in faith. In short, Brunner invites us to take the biblical language about God at face value, as the narrative of God's dealings with humankind. Since the text does not con-cern itself with a philosophical concept of God, neither should we. Rather, in encountering the divine-human relationship in the text, we are drawn up into this encounter ourselves and catch glimpses of the God who reveals himself as person.[17] But now we must turn to our final early twentieth-century argument for divine personality.

H. H. Farmer was John Oman's successor as professor of systematic theology at Westminster College, Cambridge, from 1935 to 1960 and Norris-Hulse Pro-fessor in the University of Cambridge from 1949 to 1960. The argument for con-ceiving God as person that I want to discuss briefly occurs in the text of his 1950 Gifford Lectures, published in 1954 as *Revelation and Religion: Studies in the Theological Interpretation of Religious Types.* Farmer takes as his task in the lectures an interpretation of religion from the standpoint of the distinctively Christian revelation and faith that are the basis for Christian theology. We cannot take the time now to look at the very interesting overall argument of this work but rather must zero in on his explication of the "normative concept of religion," in which he works out his argument for divine personality. It is worth noting at the outset, however, that we have here yet another starting point for examining the question of divine personality. Unlike the previous three theologians, Farmer is not working on an intra-Christian theological problem but instead is attempting to understand the world religions theologically. He comes to the conclusion early in his argument that one cannot study religion in a purely scientific way, partly because one needs empathy to understand it and partly because one is always presupposing a concept of religion in order to arrange the empirical data. It is most honest and helpful, then, to make explicit what the a priori concept looks like and where it comes from. And for a Christian philosopher of religion, it should not be a surprise that the concept comes from Christianity.[18]

Farmer maintains that to get at the normative concept of religion, one must analyze not theology or Scripture but Christian worship—especially the central act of prayer:

> [W]orship assembles together, as it were, the scattered and sporadic religious feelings, the unfocused religious sentiments, the subconscious religious convictions, which may accompany in greater or less degree the ordinary interests of life, and brings them to a unity in a single, deliberate act of attention directed towards the divine reality as such, as their object and source.[19]

For Christians, the focal point in worship is the faith that in Jesus Christ, God became incarnate. Worship of God, then, is properly directed to Jesus. And this is the reason why, for the Christian, the encounter with God is "essentially and inalterably the apprehension and encounter with Him as personal."[20] When Christians ascribe divinity to Christ, they do so through reference to the Trinitarian name of God, and any thoughtful outsider observing Christians at worship would be certain to see this. Thus, Farmer develops his discussion of the normative Christian concept of religion through successive consideration of the terms *God, Father, Son,* and *Holy Spirit.* The term *God,* according to Farmer, refers to a being who is *sui generis*—one of a kind. In worship, the Christian mind is possessed with the sense of "the sheer 'God-ness' of God."[21] Farmer is critical of the phrase "wholly other," made popular by Barth and others, as a descriptor of this quality of God. He sees it as a self-refuting assertion in the sense that if God were *wholly* other, we could not know anything about God even on the basis of his self-revelation—not even *that* God is wholly other! Revelation, on the contrary, presupposes enough likeness or "non-otherness" for a relation to be formed.

God's otherness, according to Farmer, consists primarily in two forms. His ontological otherness is God's otherness as the transcendent, absolute source of being, and in relation to God in this sense we are aware of our absolute dependence. Schleiermacher, therefore, was right to emphasize the feeling of absolute dependence as fundamental to Christian piety.[22] But there is also another sense of God's otherness, which Farmer calls his "axiological otherness." God in this way is perceived as the most real and the most perfect being. Whatever values we hold in limited measure we ascribe to God in their fullness. But more than this, God is recognized as the sole source of value and as the one whose infinite perfection not only realizes all right human values but also "includes inexhaustible ranges of value which, while not discordant with what is of the highest value for human life, nevertheless in the nature of the case cannot characterize human life; they belong solely to the distinctive being and perfection of God."[23] The believer who finds herself in the presence of God's incomparable worth cannot do other than to acknowledge her unworthiness, and no sense of achievement ever diminishes this reaction—in fact, it has the opposite effect of increasing the sense of unworthiness. In these ways, then, God may be said to be without a peer.

When he comes to the term *Father*, however, Farmer turns from God's otherness to God's intimacy as a person who enters into personal relations with human beings. He insists the term *Father* is to be taken realistically: not to do so would be as inappropriate as it would be "to compare the attraction of a magnet for iron to the relationship of friends."[24] He is critical of the Chicago theologian Henry Nelson Wieman for suggesting that while personal language for God is appropriate in worship, it is conceptually incorrect and should be acknowledged as such in theology.[25] Farmer, as far as I can tell, does not really attempt to answer the philosophical objections to the notion of an infinite or absolute person. He simply objects that the language of piety and the language of theology, or perhaps more precisely the heart and mind of the theologian, cannot be so easily divorced. And then he simply reasserts that Christians worship a personal God. He follows the assertion, however, with an important qualifier:

> In Christian worship, when it is true to itself, the awareness of the transcendent otherness of God is never submerged by the awareness of His personal nature and approach, nor is the awareness of His personal nature and approach submerged by the awareness of His transcendent otherness. Both elements are held together, and reciprocally pervade one another, in a single unitary apprehension of, and encounter with, God.[26]

Christians worship a God who is a person like no other person.

In the explication of the term *Son*, Farmer comes to the heart of the Christian's encounter with God as person, for whatever I-Thou relationship with God a Christian may experience is focused on Christ. Farmer argues that in Holy Communion, perhaps more clearly than anywhere else in Christian worship, the intimate, direct, personal relationship with God in Christ is experienced. What we receive in this relationship is the love of God: a love that gives us all, and a love that demands our all. It is in relation to God the Son, then, that the divine personality is most clearly experienced.[27]

Finally, in explication of the term *Spirit*, Farmer returns to a sense in which God is something more than or different from a person. For God as Spirit is experienced in Christian worship not as someone who is "out there," so to speak, but as the inner creative and recreative power within the believer. Farmer mentions the criticisms of the I-Thou metaphor for the divine-human encounter put forth by the psychologist C. G. Jung, the theologian Paul Tillich, and the philosopher F. H. Bradley, and he admits the force of their demurrals. But he argues that in fact the tendency to reduce everything in the Christian's awareness of God to I-Thou encounter is not the typical tendency in Christian religion. He agrees with Rudolf Otto that personal symbols for God, such as Lord, King, Father, and Judge, are balanced by impersonal but dynamic symbols, such as light, life, spirit, and fire—images that emphasize the pervading and indwelling quality of the divine presence.[28]

What can we say about these early twentieth-century arguments for divine personality? First, clearly, they begin from several different problems. For the early Barth, the issue is one of reconciling apparently irreconcilable aspects of Christian religious experience, while for the later Barth and for Brunner, the problem is how to overcome the inadequacy of human experience to rise to the knowledge of God. For Oman, the presenting problem is that of understanding the experience of moral development as a constant of human life. And for Farmer, the problem is to elicit from Christian devotional practices the implicit, normative concept of God in order to be able to look critically at the religions through the lens of Christian religion. It is clear, then, that assertion of divine personality is not the answer to a single, pressing problem in early twentieth-century theology.

One cannot help but note, however, that all four theologians were born before the First World War, and all but Oman lived past the Second. Since they were also all Europeans, situated in the theater of these horrible conflagrations, it seems only reasonable that their lives and thoughts would be shaped in many ways by that experience. Barth's reactions to both wars are well known. Brunner makes explicit reference to the First World War in *The Divine-Human Encounter*. Oman notes in the preface of *Grace and Personality* that his work as a chaplain during the First World War forced upon him a reconsideration of his whole religious position, and he goes on, "[T]he fact that such sorrow and wickedness could happen in the world, became the crucible in which my whole view of the world had to be tested."[29] Farmer, being the youngest of the four theologians, was more decisively influenced by World War II, but undoubtedly the disturbing questions that war raised for Christian theology were even more acute. I cannot help but wonder whether the massive loss of life, the suffering of the innocent, and the consequent loss of confidence in human ability to secure the value of their own lives might lie behind the arguments of all four theologians: each in his own way is seeking to reaffirm the worth of individual human life under the grace of a personal God. That said, I certainly would not wish to reduce the arguments to epiphenomena of their social contexts.

What is interesting to me is the contrast between Barth and Brunner, on the one side, and Oman and Farmer, on the other. Brunner, however much he disagreed with Barth about natural theology, on this issue joins him in asserting the absolute priority of revelation—that is, the Bible read straightforwardly—as the starting point for the knowledge of God. Farmer and Oman, on the other side, both begin with aspects of human experience. The mature Barth and

Brunner, likewise, do little to balance the picture of God as person with qualifications, while Oman and Farmer both carefully qualify their assertions:
Oman by not explicitly saying that God *is* a person, and Farmer by his emphasis on God's *sui generis* character. Now, however, we must look back to classical Reformed theology to see how faithful our twentieth-century theologians
were to the tradition.

## CALVIN AND WOLLEBIUS ON THE HIDDEN GOD

John Calvin's (1509–64) doctrine of God has been the subject of a generous
amount of scholarly debate, much of it focused on the question of the structure
of the final edition of his *Institutes of the Christian Religion*.[30] Without tarrying
over the details of that debate, we should remember what generated it: the fact
that Calvin does not develop his doctrine of God in a single *locus de deo*, as did
earlier scholastic authors, who typically covered the subject through a discussion
of the metaphysical and moral attributes of God and the doctrine of the Trinity.
Calvin, on the contrary, chooses to make the knowledge of God the theme of his
entire system of theology: first, the knowledge of God the Creator, and second,
the knowledge of God the Redeemer. Thus, it is only after one has read Calvin's
entire system of theology that one will adequately grasp the concept of God that
undergirds his Christian faith. Unfortunately, too often Calvin's interpreters—
even those who claim to be his friends and disciples—fail to understand his doctrine of God in its full richness and complexity.

While Calvin's understanding of God cannot be simply summarized, a number of key themes in it recur throughout the *Institutes*. Most striking in the argument of the opening chapters is his abhorrence of idolatry. The knowledge of
God is not an intellectual problem to be toyed with by philosophers. Its purpose
is both practical and existential: it is to orient the human person toward the true
God, in whose worship and service alone human life finds meaning and purpose.
Like Paul in the Epistle to the Romans, however, Calvin argues that humans per-
petually evade the true God who discloses himself so unmistakably in the world
and instead fashion for themselves false gods who serve to underwrite their sinful choices. The human mind, Calvin claims, is nothing short of a "factory of
idols." Now, while the tendency to idolatry is not strictly a proposition about
God but about humanity, it serves for Calvin as a critical starting point for the
doctrine of God: for, as sinful humans, theologians, too, are liable to create idols,
even under the guise of theological reflection. The antidote, Calvin claims, is
strict reliance on God's self-revelation.[31]

In the very act of revelation, however, another layer of difficulties with human
knowledge of God is disclosed. For God does not reveal himself to us directly:
Calvin takes seriously the biblical notion that no one can see God and live. Thus,
in order that finite humans can know something of God, God "accommodates"
himself to their weakness. Calvin writes:

[A]s nurses commonly do with infants, God is wont in a manner to "lisp" in speaking to us . . . [and] such forms of speaking do not so much express clearly what God is like as accommodate the knowledge of him to our slight capacity. To do this he must descend far beneath his loftiness.[32]

The concept of accommodation is used freely and in a wide variety of contexts by Calvin.[33] Scripture is an accommodation, as is the ministry of the Word and the Sacraments. If God were to speak to us directly, we would be terrified. Even the incarnation in Jesus is an accommodation.[34] In these and many other ways, God talks baby talk to us, so that we can have some impression of God's will toward us without being destroyed by him. However, it would be a mistake to take the baby talk as a literal description of God. Calvin repeatedly warns that accommodated expressions are not properly taken as divine attributes. For example, God's wrath does not describe an emotion or feeling that God in fact possesses. Rather, it is the way God makes himself appear to us so that we may know ourselves to be sinful.[35] The important conclusion that Calvin wants us to bear in mind is that human beings never know *what* God is in himself but only *how* God is to us. These are the limits beyond which the human mind cannot go.[36]

It follows from what has already been said that God is not fully disclosed by his self-revelation. Calvin has at least two ways of talking about this: God is hidden both *beyond* his revelation and *in* his revelation. First, he argues that the divine being cannot be closed in any finite form. This conviction stands behind his objections to the Lutheran understanding of the Eucharist. But it is likewise true of the incarnation: "The Son of God descended from heaven in such a way that, without leaving heaven, he willed to be borne in the virgin's womb, to go about the earth, and to hang upon the cross; yet he continuously filled the world even as he had done from the beginning."[37] Even in the person of the Mediator, God could not be contained in finite form. Second, Calvin insists with Isaiah that God is a God who hides himself.[38] Clearly, God hides himself from those who do not receive the corrective help of revelation. But even in his self-revelation, God hides as well as reveals himself. Calvin sees the evidence of this chiefly in the revelation of God in providence and predestination. For example, one infant is born to a mother who can nurse her; another is not.[39] In spite of the orderliness of nature, seemingly contingent inequalities and tragedies abound on all sides, and they seem to point to a dark side to God—a side that is unaffected by the massive and disproportionate suffering of God's creatures. If we allow our reflection to rest only on the testimony of experience, we are driven to extreme anxiety. Calvin's recommendation is to stop trying to sort out the meaning of God's providence in seemingly contingent events and rather to trust wholly the character of God as revealed in the Word.[40] This strategy does nothing, however, to deny the mysterious and inscrutable aspects of God that are disclosed in common human experience.

Perhaps even more troubling to Calvin, however, is the hiddenness of God in the "horrible decree" of double predestination.[41] Even when we turn our eyes to salvation in Christ, we become aware that not all receive the gospel when it is presented to them. Calvin thinks both Scripture and experience testify to God's eternal predestination, by which he compacts with himself what will become of every person.[42] But if the believer dwells on the fate of the reprobate, he is bound to encounter once again a God who seems, by human standards, arbitrary at best, perhaps even evil. Once again, Calvin's advice is to steer clear of speculation and to contemplate our own election as it is mirrored in Christ.[43] But the fact remains that there is much about God, even as he reveals himself in Christ, that is unknown and unknowable.

The constant refrain that one encounters in Calvin's discussion of God, then, is the warning that we must not attempt to exceed the boundaries God has established for our knowledge of himself. Speculation and vain curiosity are to be avoided. Rather, the one who would know God should cultivate a modest and sober attitude, open to the limited but sufficient insight that God gives us in his Word.[44] We might even venture to say that Calvin recommends a pious agnosticism in this sense: it is better to say, when necessary, that we do not know than to claim an overreaching insight into the divine nature. This attitude comes through very clearly in Calvin's discussion of the doctrine of the Trinity in the *Institutes,* book I, chapter 13. He applauds Augustine for recognizing that the terms of Trinitarian orthodoxy are "forced upon us by necessity, not to express what is, but only not to be silent."[45] But the very same father of the ancient church comes in for criticism in a later chapter for his psychological analogy for the Trinity: "[T]hat speculation of Augustine, that the soul is the reflection of the Trinity because in it reside the understanding, will, and memory, is by no means sound."[46] Because we do not have a firm knowledge of God in himself, we should be especially restrained in requiring others to subscribe to the words we invent to describe God.[47] Calvin inserts an extended gloss on the difficulty of forming a doctrine of God in paragraph 21:

> Here, indeed, if anywhere in the secret mysteries of Scripture, we ought to play the philosopher soberly and with great moderation; let us use great caution that neither our thoughts nor our speech go beyond the limits to which the Word of God itself extends. For how can the human mind measure off the measureless essence of God according to its own little measure, a mind as yet unable to establish for certain the nature of the sun's body, though men's eyes daily gaze upon it? Indeed, how can the mind by its own leading come to search out God's essence when it cannot even get to its own? Let us then willingly leave to God the knowledge of himself. For . . . he is the one fit witness to himself, and is not known except through himself.[48]

So does Calvin consider God a person? First, I suppose, we need to acknowledge that he never answers that question precisely. As B. A. Gerrish has argued, Calvin uses two central metaphors to describe the divine being: the Father and the fountain of every good thing.[49] One of these metaphors is personal, the other impersonal. If by "person" we mean a being who has integrated self-consciousness and who can act on the basis of willed intentions, then Calvin surely thinks of God as personal. Everything that happens occurs because of the divine will. But

Calvin is also careful to distinguish between God and human beings. God has no emotions and does not change or develop in reciprocity with his creation. God's will is eternal and stands as the ground of the finite created order. Calvin is especially careful at many points to correct the impression of reciprocity between God and human beings that seems implied in the biblical narrative. God does not change God's mind, and God owes us nothing.[50] It would require a substantial book to sort out the sources for Calvin's doctrine of God and to determine to what extent he followed his own recommendation that we must be satisfied with what we can know of God as revealed in God's Word. For now I simply venture to conclude that although Calvin thinks God possesses the spiritual powers we associate with personhood, such as consciousness and intention, he does not think of God as merely a person among other persons. God's otherness and hiddenness, as well as his attributes of eternity, omnipotence, and impassibility, all demonstrate that God does not have, in all respects, the kind of relationships that limited, definite persons have with other persons. For Calvin, God is not less than personal—that is, a force like the laws of nature (here see his argument against conceiving providence as fate)[51]—but God is also more and other than a person.

The next several generations of Reformed theologians after Calvin perhaps lacked the modesty and sobriety that he so valued as theological virtues. Often referred to as the period of Protestant scholasticism or Reformed orthodoxy, the seventeenth century saw the strict systematization of the insights of the first- and second-generation reformers. Johannes Wollebius's (1586–1629) *Compendium of Christian Theology* (1626) is one of the more influential textbooks produced in this period. Wollebius does not shy away from developing a distinct *locus de deo*. The first four chapters of his book treat in sequence the essence of God, the persons of the Godhead, the works of God, the divine decrees in general, and predestination. Wollebius argues that there are two kinds of divine attributes: communicable and incommunicable. The latter are those that no creatures share; the former are those that we share by analogy. The primary incommunicable attributes that distinguish God from all creatures are simplicity—that is, freedom from all composition—and infinity—that is, infinite being, good in every respect, and without end.[52] Wollebius understands the divine simplicity to imply that there is nothing in God that is not God himself. Therefore, whatever different features we attribute to him are not real divisions or parts of the divine will but "mere verbal distinctions."[53] There is no real difference in God between essence and existence or between will and act, and God also knows everything "in one absolutely simple act."[54] The infinity of God is not simply a maximum extension of finite existence but rather a being of a different order. "The difference between the finite and the infinite is of an altogether different order from that between a small dish and the ocean."[55] With respect to the divine decrees, he argues that "[s]uch questions as whether God first decreed this or that, and whether he decreed first the end or the means, are foolish. Since a decree of God is in itself one absolutely simple act, there is in it no earlier or later; only with respect to the things decreed can these be specified."[56] Like Calvin in discussing the incarnation in Christ, Wollebius maintains that "the infinite cannot be comprehended by the finite; the finite sees the whole God, but does not see him in his entirety."[57]

Although Wollebius's scholastic style is quite different than Calvin's, he is certainly developing, and giving further definition to, some ideas we can trace to Calvin. But if Calvin tended to focus on the negative implications of the limitations of human wisdom, Wollebius tries to infer from these negations what can be said positively about God. Calvin, for example, says that Scripture's attributions of emotions to God are accommodated expressions that tell us only what God seems like to us. Wollebius goes a step further to say that the very idea of a fluctuating and differentiated emotional life contradicts the definition of God. Therefore, we can conclude that there are no such divisions in God, that is, God is simple. Similarly, while Calvin states the negative form of the proposition "God does not change," Wollebius puts it in the positive form, "God's will is simple." The point they are making, I believe, is the same: discrete events do not occur as the result of distinct ad hoc divine intentions. Rather, everything that is exists because of the one simple and eternal divine will. Because Wollebius adopted the genre of a scholastic manual, he trimmed his citations and allusions to the biblical text to a minimum. This has the effect of making his God seem even less person-like than Calvin's. In fact, the chapters on the divine essence and the divine decrees read more like a list of careful qualifications to our concept of God than a full description. After looking at Wollebius, we might well wonder with Schleiermacher (as in my epigraph) whether it is more accurate to say that he denied personhood to God than that he asserted it.[58]

## DIVINE PERSONALITY IN
## NINETEENTH-CENTURY THEOLOGY

From the publication of his first major theological work, *On Religion: Speeches to Its Cultured Despisers* (1799), written anonymously when he was a Reformed chaplain at a Berlin hospital, Friedrich Schleiermacher had to contend with the criticism that he was promoting pantheism, and this line of objection has been urged against his theology ever since. However, if a pantheist is one who cannot maintain adequately a distinction between God and the world, then it seems clear, as I hope to demonstrate from some passages in his dogmatic masterpiece *The Christian Faith,* that Schleiermacher was no pantheist, whatever unguarded compliments he may have paid to Spinoza. What is clear is that, from his first publication and throughout his life, Schleiermacher was an outspoken critic of anthropomorphic conceptions of God.[59]

In the *Speeches,* he asserts that piety is located not in thinking or doing but in feeling—specifically, the intuition that all finite being exists in and through the infinite. As such, piety is not necessarily connected with any particular doctrinal formulation. The popular conception of God, however, draws God too much in human likeness—as a thinking and willing person who takes part in the fray of finite existence as one player. Whenever this idea is presented crudely, it is understandable that more philosophically inclined believers, having a "dread of this anthropomorphism," should substitute for it "an idea of the Highest Being, not as personally thinking and willing, but exalted above all personality, as the universal, productive, connecting necessity of all thought and existence."[60] One can be pious whether or not one holds a personal conception of God. Schleiermacher is critical of the cultured despisers for dismissing the piety of those who hold to some measure of anthropomorphism and equally critical of orthodox believers for dismissing those who reject anthropomorphism. "The rejection of the idea of a personal Deity does not decide against the presence of the deity in [a devout person's] . . . feeling. The ground of such a rejection might be a humble consciousness of the limitation of personal existence, and particularly of personality joined to consciousness."[61]

If one can be truly pious either with or without the notion of a personal God, we cannot make the notion a litmus test of piety. Atheism is not unwillingness to attribute personality to God but God-forgetfulness. Schleiermacher ends, however, by taking the side of the rejecters of anthropomorphism. He states:

> [W]hosoever insists, it matters not how many excellent men he excludes, that the highest piety consists in confessing that the Highest Being thinks as a person and wills outside the world, cannot be far travelled in the region of piety. Nay, the profoundest words of the most zealous defenders of his own faith must still be strange to him.[62]

Further, it is quite possible to believe in a personal God without piety, since one can come to the idea with mixed motives or simply "from the need for such a being to console and help."[63] In his explanations added to the third edition of the text, Schleiermacher says this more bluntly:

> The most anthropomorphic view of God usually presupposes a morally corrupt consciousness, and the same holds of such a conception of immortality as pictures the Elysian fields as just a more beautiful and wider earth. As there is a great difference between inability to think of God as in this way personal and the inability to think of a living God at all, so there is between one who does not hold such a sensuous conception of immortality and one who does not hope for any immortality.[64]

If one is interested in promoting a proper concept of God, then, one has to come up with a different term or metaphor, not personality. And this is precisely what Schleiermacher offers earlier in his explanations to speech 2: "As it is so difficult to think of a personality as truly infinite and incapable of suffering, a great distinction should be drawn between a personal God and a living God. The latter idea alone distinguishes from materialistic pantheism and atheistic blind necessity."[65] Christian piety asserts not that God is a person but that God is *living*.

In *The Christian Faith,* Schleiermacher argues that God is the "whence" of the feeling of absolute dependence. With a little introspection, anyone can discern that, while we have relative freedom and relative dependence in relation to all other finite beings, we depend in an absolute way on One who causes both us and them to be. In relation to this Being, whom we call "God," we are not in a relationship of reciprocity. We did not cause our own being, nor can we through our own freely determined actions prompt changes in God. Schleiermacher is careful to note that this "whence" of the feeling of absolute dependence is not the world, for even in relation to the totality of temporal existence we have a limited feeling of freedom: we are part of the world, and in a measure we can influence it. But God is the ground of all finite existence, and in relation to God we have no freedom, no reciprocity, only dependence.[66]

Like Calvin, Schleiermacher works out his doctrine of God throughout his entire system of theology. He takes doctrines to be first and foremost expressions of piety—that is, thematizations of our relation to God—and only secondarily as indirect descriptive statements about God and the world. In this sense, we might say, he accepts and rigorously applies Calvin's warnings about the limits of human knowledge of God. But between Calvin and Schleiermacher stands Immanuel Kant (1724–1804), and it is really in attempting a post-Kantian theology that Schleiermacher attends to the limits of human reason. For Schleiermacher, the point is that we can be more certain of statements we make about our own consciousness of finitude, sinfulness, and redemption than of statements, extrapolated from these experiences, about the nature of God. Nonetheless, Schleiermacher does offer a doctrine of God corresponding to each of the three major sections of *The Christian Faith* and organized around a discussion of the divine attributes. In part 1, he deals with the doctrine of creation as expressed in a general creature-consciousness that is both presupposed by and contained in the peculiarly Christian experience of redemption. In this part, the divine attributes he discusses are eternity, omnipresence, omnipotence, and omniscience. In the second part of the system, he discusses the consciousness of sin and grace. Corresponding to the discussion of sin are the divine attributes of holiness and justice, and corresponding to the discussion of grace are the attributes of love and wisdom. Throughout, Schleiermacher takes pains to distinguish God's manner of having these attributes from that of a finite being, and he does so chiefly by guarding against any notion of reciprocity between God and creation. God cannot be drawn into the sphere of contradictions.

At the very beginning of his discussion of the first group of attributes, Schleiermacher asserts something that echoes what we have already heard from Calvin and Wollebius: "All attributes which we ascribe to God are to be taken as denoting not something special in God, but only something special in the manner in which the feeling of absolute dependence is to be related to Him."[67] The very practice of assigning attributes to God arises because people cannot picture adequately to themselves what God is, and so in hymns and poetry they assign to God expressions that we use about finite beings. Dogmatics should be in the business of regulating these representations, "so that the anthropomorphic element, to be found more or less in all of them, and the sensuous which is mixed in with many, may be rendered as harmless as possible."[68] A major task for the doctrine of God, then, is to guard against the corrupting influence of unrestrained anthropomorphism. The key to understanding all the attributes is to recognize that God's causality, as absolute causality, is distinct from natural causality but identical with it in compass. That is to say, God works in a unique way, unlike any other finite cause, because God is not caught in the reciprocity of the web of nature. But at the same time, we have nothing to say of a God who is apart from nature either. Much like Calvin, Schleiermacher does not speak of God *in se,* in Godself.[69]

As he defines each attribute, it becomes clear how the restraining order against anthropomorphism works. God's eternity is not to be conceived as endless time but rather as "absolutely timeless causality . . . which conditions not only all that is temporal, but time itself as well."[70] Omnipresence is not endless extension but "the absolutely spaceless causality of God, which conditions not only all that is spatial, but space itself as well."[71] God's omnipotence is not unlimited power but power that is present in everything. As Schleiermacher puts it in his summary proposition, "The entire system of Nature, comprehending all times and spaces, is founded upon divine causality, which as eternal and omnipresent is in contrast to all finite causality; and . . . consequently everything for which there is a causality in God happens and becomes real."[72] There is, therefore, no distinction between potential and actual ideas of God, nor between what God wills and what God can do: in God, freedom and necessity exist in perfect harmony with each other.[73]

So far, the restraint on anthropomorphism seems extreme: in fact, it is quite hard to imagine God as a person at all given the many qualifications laid out under the preceding propositions. When he turns to the attribute of omniscience, however, Schleiermacher takes this to mean "the absolute spirituality [*Geistigkeit*] of the divine Omnipotence."[74] His concern in explicating this attribute is to distinguish God from a necessary force, such as the laws of nature or fate; omniscience is "the absolute livingness of the divine will."[75] But he is careful at the same time to argue that God's spirituality cannot be conceived as directly analogous to human spirituality. In God's thinking, there is no succession of ideas that issue in a later action. Instead, thought and action are perfectly at one. We cannot look to our own thought processes and extrapolate from them how God thinks, because that would require us to suppose that God "decides and produces by choice and deliberation, a view which from of old every form of teaching in any degree consistent has repudiated" (and here he cites John of Damascus!).[76] If we have to begin with an anthropomorphic image, Schleiermacher suggests,

> it would have been far safer . . . to transfer to God, illimited and perfect, the certainty of the perfect artist, who in a state of inspired discovery thinks of nothing else, to whom nothing else offers itself save what he actually produces. This also agrees very well with the story of the Creation, which knows

nothing of any intervening deliberation and deciding choice, but keeps contemplation entirely to the end, where it appears simply as absolute approval, without ascribing to God any contemplation of what He did not make or any comparison of the real world with those possible worlds.[77]

In dealing with the attributes corresponding to the consciousness of sin, Schleiermacher defines God's holiness as "that divine causality through which in all corporate human life conscience is found conjoined with the need of redemption,"[78] and God's justice is "that divine causality through which in the state of universal sinfulness there is ordained a connexion between evil and actual sin."[79] Worth noting is that these definitions avoid entirely the assumption that these attributes correspond to distinct affective states in God; rather, they speak about God's establishment of moral order in the creation, through the implantation of conscience and its yearning for something better, and through the establishment of consequences for sinful behavior. In his exposition of the attribute of holiness, he argues that the popular interpretation of God's holiness—his pleasure in goodness and displeasure with sin—cannot be taken strictly. Any feeling of pleasure or displeasure implies passivity, since the feeling arises in response to what another does or does not do. To conceive of God's holiness in this way is to disturb our feeling of absolute dependence, because "a divine state would then be determined by human action, and thus the relation between God and man so far become one of reciprocity."[80] Here anthropomorphism has gone too far and impairs the doctrine of God. In an appendix to this section, Schleiermacher rejects the notion of mercy as an attribute of God for similar reasons: it is impossible to conceive it without God's being drawn into the sphere of reciprocity.[81]

In discussing the final attributes of love and wisdom, Schleiermacher notes that love alone "is made the equivalent of the being [*Sein*] or essence [*Wesen*] of God" (he cites 1 John 4:16).[82] The other attributes already discussed cannot stand in the place of the name "God," but love can. Indeed, Schleiermacher goes so far as to say that "belief in God as almighty and eternal is nothing more than that shadow of faith which even devils may have."[83] But what does it mean that God is love? Schleiermacher takes divine love as "the attribute in virtue of which the divine nature communicates itself [*sich mitteilt*]," and it is seen in the work of redemption.[84] The divine wisdom "is the principle which orders and determines the world for the divine self-communication which is evinced in redemption."[85] The whole world as given is arranged effectively to attain this loving purpose of God to communicate himself with us. The world is a theater of redemption and the absolute revelation of the Supreme Being.[86] Returning to the metaphor he suggested in the discussion of omniscience, Schleiermacher argues that the whole world is a divine artwork—perfectly conceived, brilliantly and efficiently executed. As the self-communication of a loving God, the world as a whole is good.[87] Interestingly, Schleiermacher does not inveigh against anthropomorphism so much in his exposition of love and wisdom.

Schleiermacher nowhere says in *The Christian Faith* that God is not a person. He is very clear, however, that God cannot be conceived as one cause among others, or else we have no reason for confidence in God as the source of the feeling of absolute dependence. If God exists outside the reciprocal causality of the nature system, God does not therefore cease to be involved. God's causality is both totally other and everywhere present. God has attributes that could be conceived as analogous to human attributes, but the analogy breaks down when we explicate the meaning of God's unique causality in relation to each attribute. Although he allows for the inevitability of personal language for God—even its necessity, as my epigraph suggests—Schleiermacher believes dogmatic theology contributes most when it seeks to train and discipline anthropomorphism so that it does not lead to superstition or lack of faith.

Alois Emanuel Biedermann (1819–85) was a Reformed pastor and professor of theology at the University of Zurich from 1850 to 1885. Already in 1842, Biedermann had jumped into the fray on what had become a very controversial question in German theology—namely, the possibility of conceiving of God as a person—with a review article in which he defended David Friedrich Strauss's unorthodox views against one of his published critics.[88] By the time of the publication of his *Christian Dogmatics* in 1869, Biedermann had worked out his own careful critique of the notion that God is a person. He adopted from Hegel the distinction between representational and conceptual language. In his dogmatics he attempts to critique the representations of religious perception as given in church dogma and to raise them speculatively to pure concepts that are not in conflict with scientific thought. This is not in order to replace representational thinking in the practice of religion but rather to restrain its potential to mislead.[89]

Biedermann argues that the concept "absolute spirit" contains everything essential in the idea of God, so that if we grasp it purely, we have the right concept of God. He argues that among theists, the "controversy over the 'personality' of God is only a verbal dispute" in the sense that those who call God a person do not wish to suggest that he is finite, and those who deny God's personhood do not wish to deny God's spirituality. Nonetheless, like Schleiermacher, Biedermann thinks the controversy should be decided for the denial, since "the concept of personality cannot be so stripped off from finite spirit that there would at the same time be an abstraction from the elements of finitude."[90] Personality is, in fact, the specific form of finite spirit—its limitation in a specific, discrete individual. But spirit is by definition infinite—it is without being here or there, it exists in and of itself. Therefore, Biedermann concludes that only absolute spirit is an adequate conceptualization of God for pure thought. He does not disallow, however, the necessity for representation to view God as person. The duty of the speculative theologian is to make clear what is and is not strictly true in representational thought, so that our language and images do not mislead us. But we can confidently continue to relate to God as personal in our individual and corporate piety. Biedermann concludes:

> Only man as finite spirit is personality; God as absolute spirit is not. Yet the religious intercourse is always a personal one, and indeed not merely in subjective representation but in objective truth, because it goes on between the

infinite and the finite spirit within the finite human spiritual life and thus must take place throughout in the form of the latter.[91]

Although he has picked up some terminology from Hegel, I see Biedermann's approach as very similar to Schleiermacher's. The task of the dogmatic theologian is to restrain anthropomorphism, not to eliminate it. Biedermann, however, asserts more bluntly that God is not a person, since personhood is by definition finite. The representational language of piety is unavoidable and it cannot be dispensed with. But only the most unreflective person would take this language for a pure description of God.

## CONCLUSION

What can we say, then, after this whirlwind tour of Reformed theologians' views on the personality of God? It seems clear that the nineteenth- and the twentieth-century theologians, respectively, represent two very different trajectories from the received tradition. Schleiermacher and Biedermann are more inclined to press the tradition's emphasis on the limits of human language for God and insistence that there are no real distinctions within the Godhead. This leads them to a state of relative discomfort with anthropomorphism and to an emphasis on the need to restrain and discipline metaphors taken from the realm of human experience. Our twentieth-century theologians, by contrast, each for different reasons, tended to retrieve the personal language and imagery that the older theologians unselfconsciously passed on from Scripture. Barth, Brunner, and Farmer also appeal to a Christocentric understanding of revelation as additional justification for their strong emphasis on the experience of God as an I-Thou encounter.

It is worth noting, however, that the representatives of both trajectories of the tradition tip their hats to the other side. On the one hand, the early Barth, with his notion of God as "the Exalted One," recognized that personality could not say all that needed to be said about God. So, too, Farmer, with his emphasis on the "sheer God-ness of God"—God's *sui generis* character—as well as his understanding of the immanence of the Spirit, clearly indicated that divine personality needs to be qualified by other descriptions. In fact, his repeated claim that God is unique in his class tends to undermine whatever analogies one could draw between divine and human persons. On the other hand, Schleiermacher and Biedermann both recognized and acknowledged the need for piety to represent God as personal. It is difficult to imagine, they both contended, how Christians could pray and worship God without such images. The important thing is to remember that we formulate the images because we need them, not because we have direct insight into God's being.

I conclude by suggesting why I believe the time has come for us to rethink the somewhat novel approach of twentieth-century theologians on divine personality. For at least three reasons, I believe the tendency toward intensifying personal language for God is now misguided, however necessary or understandable it was in its own context. First, the increased emphasis on divine personality that we saw at work in the twentieth century greatly exacerbates the problem of evil. I certainly experienced that in my hospital bed twenty-odd years ago. The new orthodoxy of the twentieth century, with titles such as *The Crucified God* and *Narratives of a Vulnerable God*, seems to be that God is our co-sufferer.[92] Whatever one can say about this resolution of the problem of evil (if it is one), we can certainly affirm that it would have been shockingly unorthodox—even heretical—to our Christian forebears from every century but the last. Is it possible to retain a concept of God as a good person, vulnerable to pain, without implying that God, like other good persons, is finite?

A second problem with the intensified emphasis on divine personhood has to do with the interface between theology and science, for it is clearly the notion of a personal God that leads many scientists to forswear religion. Can it be that we have forced a choice between faith and science? Many scientists object to the notion of a personal God who intervenes in nature and history because it is disruptive of the faith in the orderliness of the laws of nature that scientific research presupposes.[93] A concept of divine activity as strictly analogous to human activity undermines that confidence, because one can never predict what God will do next in reaction to one person or situation and another.

The final problem is perhaps the most serious one of all. Intensified personal language for God may encourage us to imagine that God is at our disposal or to project onto God our own favorite wishes and highest values; in other words, it may lure us into a form of idolatry. God is not less than a person; God is certainly much more, and our experience of God cannot be reduced to an I-Thou encounter. The God who is "without body, parts, or passions," to quote the Westminster Confession, is a God who is "alone in and unto himself all-sufficient, not standing in need of any creatures," and yet he is also "alone fountain of all being, of whom, through whom, and to whom, are all things."[94] For this reason, too, a Reformed doctrine of God for this new century and millennium will need to remember its roots in the awe, modesty, and pious agnosticism of Calvin, which will surely nurture a more reverent piety than the uncritical anthropomorphism fostered by popular religion.[95]

# Chapter 5

# Justice and Justification
*Nicholas Wolterstorff*

> *Since human beings bear the image of God engraven on them, God deems himself violated in their person.... This doctrine is to be carefully observed, that no one can be injurious to his brother without wounding God himself. Were this doctrine deeply fixed in our minds, we should be much more reluctant than we are to inflict injuries.*
>
> —Calvin, Commentary on Genesis 9:5–6

What do justice and justification have to do with each other—if anything? That is my topic. By "justification" I mean, of course, that act of God most prominently featured in those two great letters of St. Paul, his letter to the Romans and his letter to the Galatians. And by "justice" I mean a certain relationship among persons; I'll offer some analysis later as to the nature of that relationship. What do these two things, God's act of justification and just relationships among persons, have to do with each other?

It appears to me to be commonly taken for granted that they have little to do with each other. Everybody, if pressed, would concede that they have *some* relation to each other; most everything does have some relation to most everything else. But the relation is assumed to be attenuated—scarcely worth taking note of. Social ethicists talk about justice; theologians, about justification; few, about both.[1]

Is it plausible to assume that they have nothing much to do with each other? In Deuteronomy 10:18, the speaker, Moses, says that God "executes justice for the fatherless and the widow, and loves the sojourner, giving him food and clothing" (RSV); he then goes on to say that Israel is to do likewise. Many other passages from the Old Testament could be cited to the same effect. Is it purely

accidental that Paul would use the same word, in its verbal rather than nomina-
tive form, to speak of the believer's status before God as the result of Christ's
work? The believer, he says, is *justified*. The Bible wasn't written in English; to
make what I just said *strictly speaking* true, I would have to rephrase it with that
in mind.

## ON TRANSLATING PAUL

Let me get into the issues by raising a question as to how we should translate into
English a cluster of words having a certain common stem in Paul's letters to the
Romans and to the Galatians. I raise the question by scrutinizing the Revised
Standard Version's translation of Romans. I choose this translation for two reasons. First, it appears to me that in spite of a flurry of other translations it, along
with its successor, the New Revised Standard Version, is probably still the most
widely used English translation of the Bible.[2] Second, it enables me to raise the
question I want to raise as effectively as does any other translation. When I have
finished looking at how the RSV handles the issue, I will look briefly at how some
other recent English translations handle it.

The Greek text of Romans 1 through 10 is littered with grammatical variants
on the *dikai-* stem; over and over we find the adjective *dikaios*, the noun *dikaiosunê*, and the verb *dikaioô*. When I, as a sometime reader of classical Greek,
approach an English translation of this passage, I expect this adjective, noun, and
verb to be translated, respectively, as "just," "justice," and "to justify." That's how
they would standardly be translated in classical Greek. What I find instead is a
near-relentless drive to avoid translating the adjective and the noun thus. Almost
always the adjective is translated as "righteous" and the noun as "righteousness."
Indeed, I find this near-relentless drive—to avoid translating grammatical variants on the *dikai-* stem with grammatical variants on the English *just*—operative
in the RSV translation of the New Testament generally; usually, though not
always, the translation of choice is a grammatical variant on our word *righteous*.
To cite just one example of this drive at work: in the Beatitudes as we find them
in Matthew 5, we read, "Blessed are those who hunger and thirst for *dikaiosunê*,
for they will be satisfied" and "Blessed are those who are persecuted for the sake
of *dikaiosunê*, for theirs is the kingdom of heaven." In both cases, *dikaiosunê* is
translated by the RSV as "righteousness."

Back to Romans. What I called the near-relentless drive to avoid translating
words having the *dikai-* stem with grammatical variants on our word "just" is
reined in when the translators come to the verb form, *dikaioô*. This is consistently
translated with our English verb "justify." The result of this discrepancy, translating the adjective and noun one way and the verb another, is that the linguistic structure which leaps out in the Greek is completely obscured for the English
reader. I could illustrate the point with any number of passages. Let me cite the
RSV translation of Romans 3:21–26, since I will be making reference to it later:

But now the righteousness of God has been manifested apart from law, although the law and the prophets bear witness to it, the righteousness of God through faith in Jesus Christ for all who believe. For there is no distinction; since all have sinned and fall short of the glory of God, they are justified by his grace as a gift through the redemption which is in Christ Jesus, whom God put forward as an expiation by his blood, to be received by faith. This was to show God's righteousness, because in his divine forbearance he had passed over former sins; it was to prove at the present time that he himself is righteous and that he justifies him who has faith in Jesus.

The single occurrence in this passage of the adjective *dikaios* is translated with "righteous," and the triple occurrence of the noun *dikaiosunê* is translated each time with "righteousness"; but the double occurrence of the verb *dikaioô* is translated both times with the verb "justify."

Why the difference? Why did that near-relentless drive get reined in when it came to the Greek verb? I do not know; I can only speculate. One possibility—not very plausible to my mind—is that the translators couldn't think of an English verb with the same stem as "righteous" and "righteousness." If that was the case, some recent translators and commentators help them out by employing the verb "rectify"; what God does in Christ is rectify us. I am thinking here especially of Louis Martyn's commentary on Galatians.[3]

As I say, I don't find this speculation very plausible; it takes no deep acquaintance with the English language to know that "rectify" is the verbal form of "righteous" and "righteousness." My guess is that what was instead operative was the translators' commitment to a certain Protestant understanding of what Paul meant by "justification," coupled with their reluctance to collide with the fact that the expression "justification by faith" has been central in the English-language formulation of that theology. It's also my guess that it was that same tradition of Protestant theology that led the translators to translate the adjective *dikaios* as "righteous" and the noun *dikaiosunê* as "righteousness"; but we'll get to that later.

Whatever the reason, the drive to avoid translating *dikai-* stem words with grammatical variants on our word "just" gets reined in when confronted with the verb; until that time it is, I said, *near*-relentless. Why it's not *fully* relentless until it gets reined in when confronted with the verb is completely obscure to me. In any case, the fact that it's not fully relentless until then confronts the English reader every now and then with even more textual disarray than that resulting from the fact that the verb is translated differently from the noun and adjective.

Let me illustrate. In Romans 3:5, Paul asks, in the RSV translation, "But if our wickedness serves to show the justice of God, what shall we say? That God is unjust to inflict wrath on us?" The Greek word translated as "justice" is, of course, *dikaiosunê*, and the word translated as "unjust" is *adikos*. After developing the thought that God would not be unjust should God inflict God's wrath on us, Paul begins his description in verse 21 of the new order of things with the words, in the RSV translation, "But now the righteousness of God has been manifested apart from law. . . ." The Greek noun is again *dikaiosunê*, but this time it gets translated as "righteousness." The result of this discrepancy in translation is that to the English reader a contrast is suggested between God's "attribute" in the old order and God's "attribute" in the new order: where previously it was God's justice that confronted us, now it is God's righteousness. In the Greek text there is no such contrast; in both the old order and the new, it is God's *dikaiosunê* that is manifested.

Another, to my mind even worse, example of the textual disarray produced by this inconsistency in translating even the noun *dikaiosunê* occurs at the beginning of chapter 4 of Romans, verses 1 through 12. Speaking of Abraham's justification, Paul six times over uses, in the RSV, the verbal phrase "reckons X to Y as righteousness," as in "Abraham's faith was reckoned to him as righteousness." I think it's clear that Paul is using the verbal phrase "reckons as *dikaiosunê*" as a near-synonym of the Greek verb *dikaioô*, which gets translated here as "justifies," and that the function of the more complex verbal phrase "reckons X to Y as *dikaiosunê*" is that it incorporates a reference to the person and to the ground of the reckoning. In 4:22–25, the two are used in direct parallel with each other:

> That is why [Abraham's] faith was "reckoned to him as righteousness [*dikaiosunê*]." But the words, "it was reckoned to him," were written not for his sake alone, but for ours also. It will be reckoned to us who believe in him that raised from the dead Jesus our Lord, who was put to death for our trespasses and raised for our justification.

Whether I'm right or wrong about the near-synonymy of "reckons as *dikaiosunê*" with "*dikaioô*," the verbal unity in the Greek text between the verb *dikaioô* and the phrase "reckon as *dikaiosunê*" is destroyed for the English reader by the fact that the RSV translates the verb as "justifies" and the verbal phrase as "reckons as righteousness." The disarray is particularly jarring in 4:5, which gets translated thus:

> And to one who does not work but trusts him who justifies the ungodly, his faith is reckoned as righteousness.

The Greek here is the verb *dikaioô* and the noun *dikaiosunê*.

A possible response at this point would be that this is a big fuss about nothing: "justice" and "righteousness," "just" and "righteous," "to justify" and "to rectify"—what's the difference? They all mean the same thing.

Well, in the first place it seems to me that the only plausible explanation of what led the RSV translators to translate as they did is that *they* did not view these as meaning the same thing. Had that been their view, surely they would have preserved for the English reader the verbal pattern that we find in the Greek. Either they would consistently have used grammatical variants on our word "right" or they would consistently have used grammatical variants on our word "just." And it wouldn't have made any difference which option they chose; toss a coin. Or perhaps the wish not to collide with the language traditionally used in English for expressing a certain strand of Protestant theology would have been a reason for choosing "justification by faith" over "rectification by faith." If so, that would be a reason for translating all the *dikai-* stem words with grammatical variants on our word "just"—thus preserving for the English reader the very striking pattern in Paul's Greek.

But the translators did not do that. So I surmise that they did not regard "righteous" and "just," "righteousness" and "justice," "rectify" and "justify" as synonyms. And not regarding them as synonyms, their understanding of Paul's theology was what then led them to translate as they did. They wanted to steer the reader away from the thought that Paul is talking about justice to the thought that he is speaking about *righteousness*, and about how we become righteous, namely, by being *reckoned* as righteous—which, then, is how they understand being *justified*.

You will have gathered that in my judgment it was a serious mistake for the translators to have destroyed for the English reader the textual unity of Paul's thought. I am not so naive as to suppose that every verbal pattern in an original can be preserved in a translation, nor so naive as to suppose that one can translate a text in the absence of views as to what is being said in the text; but here the imposition of a theological understanding of what's said is too blatant, too distorting, too destructive. Either stick with "righteous," "righteousness," and "rectify" or stick with "just," "justice," and "justify"; do not move back and forth at one's own discretion.

I think the translators were correct in the view I have speculatively attributed to them, namely, that these words are not synonymous; so let me now go on to argue that Paul's thought is best transmitted to us in English with the use of "just," "justice," and "justify." I concede that these words, in contemporary English, carry certain connotations that give a wrong "feel" to what Paul is saying. The "justice" family of words, in their contemporary usage, often bring judicial procedures to mind; that suggestion has to be eliminated. It's not that, in Paul's usage, words with the *dikai-* stem have nothing to do with judicial procedures; it's rather that *dikaiosunê* has to do with social relations in general, not only with those that become the subject of judicial procedures. We have to work with the notion of a relationship being just and of a person being just.

So, yes; "just," "justice," and "justify" have some misleading connotations. But surely the same is true for "righteous," "righteousness," and "rectify." In contemporary English, calling someone "righteous" carries the suggestion of *self-righteous*; for those who prefer translating Paul with this family of words, that's definitely misleading. It should also be noted that in standard English it is situations that we rectify, not persons, and that the word "righteous" is now scarcely used outside of religious contexts. Either way, then, we're dealing with misleading connotations. My argument will be that the root sense of the English "just" is exactly what's needed here to communicate Paul's thought. For one thing—this anticipates the outcome of my argument—the "righteousness" translation of Paul's thought imports an individualism and subjectivity that is simply not there.

## AN EXCURSION INTO MORAL THEORY

To advance, we'll have to take a brief excursion into moral theory. Begin with the category of the good—or, in contemporary English, better called, I think, *the excellent*. What I have in mind by "the excellent" is that which is worthy of approbation, approbation being understood as coming in many different forms: praise, worship, love, desire, and so forth. When I say that the excellent is that which is worthy of approbation, I must not be understood as offering a definition. As a definition, what I said would be circular; to say that something is worthy of approbation is to say that approbation of it is a good thing, that is, an excellent thing.

Among the things that are excellent are certain sunsets, certain governments, certain works of music, certain games, certain computers—and, of course, certain actions. Let's focus on these last: excellent actions. For a given person at a given time there are, within the set of excellent actions, those that the person is morally obligated to perform—morally bound, morally required. Required to perform on pain of what? On pain of impairment of that person's moral character. An action is morally required of one if one's failure to perform it constitutes, or would constitute, an impairment of one's moral character.

We are all aware of the fact, however, that of the actions we did perform, only some were such that we were obligated to perform them; and that of those we now can perform, only some are such that we are obligated to perform them. Some of the ones we did perform that were not obligatory were, sad to say, ones that we were obligated *not* to perform. But in addition, there were many that it was quite permissible for us not to have performed. Of those that were permissible but not obligatory, some were pretty much indifferent as to excellence; but some were truly excellent—above and beyond the call of duty, as we say, supererogatory.

I said that failure to do what one is morally obligated to do constitutes impairment of one's moral character. Let me be more pointed in my description: it constitutes guilt. Guilt is the dark side of obligation. If one fails to do what one ought to do, one is guilty. Though performance of the supererogatory act enhances one's moral character, failure of performance does not make one guilty.

How, conversely, are we to describe the person who has done what she ought to have done? She's a *good* person; or to use the old-fashioned language, she is *righteous*. She has done the right thing, that is, the obligatory thing. The fully righteous person is the one who has done all that is morally required of her. If there are laws specifying her obligations, then the righteous person is the one who has done all that the law requires.

What we have so far is the good and the right, that is to say, the excellent and the obligatory, with the obligatory being a special case of the excellent. And that is where many theorists of moral excellence call it off. I have come to believe, however, that to call it off there is to ignore another, enormously important dimension of the moral—a dimension distinct from the obligatory, though interacting with it and just as important and fundamental.

For each of us it is the case that in addition to certain actions being morally required of us, there are certain goods to which we are morally *entitled;* or, in other words, certain goods to which we have a *right*, that is, a *moral* right, a right grounded in morality.

I have learned that most people, when they hear the word "rights," think immediately of those high and lofty things that have come to be known as "natural human rights"; and I have learned that some of these, in turn, are of the view that there are no such rights. Alisdair MacIntyre is perhaps the best known of the latter group. Natural rights, he holds, are an invention of the Enlightenment—not a *discovery*; an *invention*. Such rights as there are, are confined to privileges conferred on specified groups of people by positive human law or lawlike custom. Rights are the creatures of social facts and performances.

Here is not the place for me to mount my case against this denial of natural rights. I must confine myself to urging that we not begin our reflections on rights by thinking about natural human rights but by recognizing that rights belong to the fine texture of all human interactions. To imagine the deletion of that fine texture of rights is to be left with interactions that would scarcely pass for human. Let me give one or two simple examples. If you are a student of mine and have written a top-notch paper for the course, then you have a right to my awarding you an A for the paper; and if I give you less than an A for the paper, you then have a right to my giving you a hearing on the matter. If your writing a top-notch paper did not give you the right to an A from me, then presumably what you would do is try to charm or threaten me into giving you an A; and if your telling me that you sincerely and reflectively believe there are merits in the paper that went undetected by me did not give you the right to a hearing by me, then presumably you would try to wheedle me into giving you a hearing. A society completely absent of claims based on rights, laced through and through instead with charming, threatening, and wheedling, would be Hobbes's state of nature.

I said that the dark side of obligation is guilt. Is there likewise a dark side of rights? Suppose you fail to enjoy your right to some good or other. What, then, is your condition? Not guilt, obviously; it may be that someone else is guilty for your being in the situation of not enjoying what you have a right to. But it's that person who's guilty, not you. Your condition is that you have been *wronged*—or, to speak metaphorically, that you have been wounded, morally wounded, morally injured. The dark side of rights is being wronged.

Being guilty and being wronged are obviously two fundamentally different moral phenomena. And I think it is especially the difference between these two phenomena, between *being guilty* and *being wronged,* that makes it clear that in the distinction between obligations and rights we are dealing with two distinct dimensions of the moral order.

I have been speaking as if obligations and rights were two independent, albeit interacting, dimensions of the moral order, each dependent in its own way on the good. In fact, I'm inclined to think that's not true. Contrary to the line of thought one finds in most theorists, it appears to me that rights are, in a certain way, deeper in the moral order than obligations. Justice is deeper than righteousness.

What I have in mind is this: whenever one is guilty, one is guilty *of* something. And always, what one is guilty of is having wronged someone—that someone possibly being oneself.[4] It is always *on account of* having wronged someone, *by virtue of* having wronged someone, that one is guilty. One's having wronged the person is what *grounds* one's guilt. Wronging someone is, in that way, deeper than guilt. Here are two dimensions of the moral life, being wronged and being guilty, with the latter grounded in the former, which is thus deeper than the latter. In the case of so-called perfect duties, one is guilty on account of having deprived someone of what they had a right to, thereby wronging them. In the case of so-called imperfect duties—duties of charity, for example—one is guilty not on account of having violated the rights of the person to whom one failed to extend charity but on account of having wronged God, whose command it was that one act mercifully.

And now, let's bring justice into the picture; or, more precisely, let's take note of the fact that justice has for quite some time already been in the picture. We are all familiar with the traditional formula for justice, going back into antiquity: justice is present when people enjoy or possess what's due them; injustice, when they fail to enjoy or possess what's due them. What's due a person is what that person has a right to, that is, a title to—or, in the case of retributive justice, what's due a person is what they deserve, what they have a desert to. Justice is present in relations among persons insofar as they possess or experience the goods to which they have a right or the "evils" to which they have a desert; injustice, insofar as they are wronged.

Putting everything together, what we have is this: within the moral realm are two distinct, though by no means independent, dimensions—duty and what's due one, responsibilities and rights/deserts, righteousness and justice. Righteousness is fully present when no one is guilty. Justice is fully present when no one is wronged. The two are related but distinct.

## PAUL'S TEACHING ON JUSTIFICATION

With this distinction between righteousness and justice in hand, let's go back to Paul's teaching concerning justification. What is it that Paul is wrestling with in Romans, righteousness or justice? Is guilt the problem or moral wrongs? Is Paul asking how we can become righteous or how we can become just?

Let it be said at once that it's not really a sharp either/or. The question is, which of these is at the center of Paul's thought? Given the intertwinement of righteousness and justice, whatever Paul says about the one will perforce have implications for the other. But which of the two does Paul have his eye on? Which does he regard as the central problem, being guilty or being wronged? Recall the opening lines of the wonderful African American spiritual:

> There is a balm in Gilead
> To make the wounded whole;
> There is a balm in Gilead
> To heal the sin-sick soul.

Which has priority in Paul's teaching on justification, the second line or the fourth?

My guess is that some readers will be feeling acutely uncomfortable at this point. Am I not pressing a distinction that was neither present in Paul's mind nor in the background framework that he was taking for granted? I acknowledge this as something to worry about. Note, however, that it cannot be offered as an objection by those who are happy with the RSV translation. That translation is quite clearly the production of translators who interpreted Paul as talking about righteousness and guilt, not about justice and being wronged.

I think perhaps the best way into the issue is to pose the following question. Suppose, for the moment, that at the center of Paul's attention is our moral condition of guilt. What's that to God? Why is our guilt of such concern to God that God would be angry about it and send God's own Son to redeem us from our guilt? It will be said that guilt consists in the violation of God's law—whether that law be presented to a particular person in the form of natural moral law or in the form of Torah (Rom. 2:14–15). Yes, that's certainly true. But why is our violation of God's law such a big deal for God?

Our guilt has brought about a breach between God and humankind, and God earnestly desires reconciliation; isn't that the issue? Yes, that's certainly fundamental in Paul's thought. In Romans 5:10–11, Paul speaks of our being reconciled to God through the death of God's Son; and in 5:1 he says that we who are justified by faith now have peace with God. But what does guilt have to do with that breach? And how exactly does undoing the guilt, if that's what justification achieves, effect reconciliation? Consider a human analogy: if you are guilty of one thing and another, that does not, as such, constitute any particular breach in your and my relationship. It may well evoke sorrow or dismay on my part for you, but not, as such, a breach in our relationship that calls for repair.

The reply will be forthcoming: it would be a breach in our relationship if what you're guilty of is disobeying some command or request of mine. Yes, indeed. But why exactly would that make a difference? Surely the answer is that it would make a difference because, if it's a legitimate command or request, then, other things being equal, I have a right to have my command or request honored. If you deny me that right, I have then been wronged.

I see no way of avoiding the conclusion that the reason our moral condition matters to God is that God has been wronged by what we have done. The whole world, says Paul, is "accountable to God" (Rom. 3:19). We have acted unjustly toward God; we have violated God's rights. Yes, we're guilty; yes, we're unrighteous. But the fundamental problem is that we have wronged God. That's why there's been a breach between God and us that needs healing; that's why reconciliation is called for. When you are wronged by me, then in the very nature of the case there is a breach between us, a moral breach. That's why it is appropriate for God to be angry: when I have wronged you, then it is appropriate for you to feel angry with me.

Justification, as Paul presents it, is God's way of dealing with the wrongs God has suffered at our hands. It's not God's way of dealing with our human moral condition as such. It's God's way of dealing with our moral relationship to God, specifically, with our having morally wounded God. That has implications for guilt—no doubt about it. But justification in Christ is not, first of all, God's way of dealing with that malformation *within* each of us that is our guilt but God's way of dealing with that malformation *between* us and God that consists in God's being wounded by our acts of injustice vis à vis God. Justification in Christ is God's way of dealing with the fact that we have violated God's rights.

## BECOMING A JUST PERSON

What is that way? Best to begin by having before us a way of being justified that contrasts with that new and astonishing way that Paul presents to his readers. In Romans 2, one of the points Paul makes to his fellow Jews is that merely *having* the law, that is, the Torah, is by no means sufficient for making them just vis à vis God. It is not, he says (2:13–14), "the hearers of the law who are just before God, but the doers of the law who will be justified." And then he adds, "When the Gentiles who have not the law do by nature what the law requires, they are a law to themselves. . . . They show that what the law requires is written on their hearts" (RSV).

So that's one way to be justified: if one is a Jew, to obey the Torah; if one is a Gentile, to obey the natural moral law, the content of this being the same as some of the content of the Torah. And notice what *to be justified* has to mean here. *To be justified* is *to become just*. To be justified is not to be declared or pronounced just; it's not to be treated as if one were just. It is to become just.[5] And one way to become just is always to do what justice requires.

But it is Paul's deep and firm conviction that nobody has, in fact, become just in this way. No Jew has fully obeyed the requirements of God's Torah; no Gentile has fully obeyed the requirements of God's natural moral law. God has been wronged by all of us, for the requirements of Torah and natural law are what *God requires* of us, his human children. "No human being," says Paul, "will be justified in [God's] sight by works of the law." As a matter of fact, what comes about by way of having God's requirements in our midst is not that some of us become just by obeying them but that all of us thereby acquire "knowledge of sin" (3:20 RSV). In this situation, it's not unjust that God would be angry with us (3:5); that's no violation of our rights. As already mentioned, it's true in general that anger is an appropriate response to being wronged.

And now for God's new strategy. It is stated by Paul with extreme compactness in Romans 3:21–26, the passage I cited earlier to illustrate my charge that the tight textual unity we find in Paul's thought in the original Greek is destroyed by the RSV translators. Let me state in my own words what I take Paul's thought to be—amplifying it somewhat beyond what he explicitly says here.

Paul introduces his description of God's new strategy for our becoming just by saying that it is a manifestation of the *justice* of God: "But now the justice of God has been manifested apart from law" (3:21). He says it again as he concludes his description of the new strategy: "This was to show God's justice, . . . it was to prove at the present time that [God] is just, and that [God] justifies him who has faith in Jesus" (3:25–26). The same point was already made near the beginning of the letter, when Paul was setting out on his discussion: in the gospel, he said, "the justice of God is revealed through faith for faith" (1:17).

I find this very striking indeed. God's inauguration of a new way of our becoming just does not represent the abrogation or supersession of God's justice by something superior to justice: mercy, grace, or whatever. Let it be said emphatically that it does represent mercy and grace on God's part. In 3:24, Paul says that we are "justified by God's grace as a gift, through the redemption which is in Christ Jesus" (RSV). But what Paul is saying here is not that God's justice is superseded by God's mercy but that it was an act of grace and mercy on God's part to inaugurate this new way of our becoming just and of God's justice being satisfied. This new way is at one and the same time an act of God's grace and a manifestation of *God's justice*—of God's *dikaiosunê*.

One implication of this is that this new strategy for our becoming just does not consist of God *forgiving* us. Forgiving someone for their having wronged you—and one forgives someone not for their guilt but for their having wronged one—is indeed one way of effecting reconciliation. And obviously, it's fundamental in Christian thought and experience. But forgiving someone is not a way of making them just. Forgiveness cannot do that.

I'm disagreeing here with my good friend Louis Martyn, whose commentary on Galatians I greatly admire; I dare say I'm also disagreeing with numerous other biblical scholars and theologians. But I cannot see that Paul is saying anything at all in this passage about forgiveness.[6] Martyn prefers translating all the *dikai-* stem words in Romans and Galatians with grammatical variants on our word "right." Speaking then of God's "rectifying forgiveness," he says that "what makes transgressing members of God's people right is God's forgiveness" (266). And again: "God's deed of rectification is God's merciful forgiveness of transgressions for which atonement has been made" (267). The only passage in Romans or Galatians that Martyn cites in support of this is Romans 3:25. The RSV translates the passage this way: "This was to show God's righteousness, because in his divine forbearance he had passed over former sins." Martyn translates it this way: "God did this to demonstrate the power of his rectitude; in his divine forbearance, that is to say, he has forgiven the sins previously committed" (265). The question is whether Paul is saying that God *forgave* prior sins or whether he is making the vaguer and more general claim that God *passed over* prior sins. The Greek is the noun *paresis*, and my lexicon (Thayer's *Greek-English Lexicon of the New Testament*) offers "passing over, letting pass, neglecting, disregarding" as its meaning. Forgiving sins is indeed *compatible* with passing over them; more precisely, forgiving them is one way of passing over them. But it strikes me as overinterpreting to say that Paul is here *saying* that God forgives sins.

Once again then: Paul presents God's inauguration of this new way of our becoming just as a new manifestation of God's justice. It is both at once: a new way of our becoming just and a new manifestation of God's justice. And let us not forget that it is also an exercise of mercy on God's part. It is all three at once. What, then, is this new way?

As far as I can see, it's this: God has sent/accepted Jesus Christ as the representative of humankind—representative in the following strong sense. What Christ does is done on our behalf—not unlike the way in which an ambassador acts on behalf of his government. And what Christ undergoes is undergone on our behalf—not unlike a parent paying a fine on behalf of his or her child. Thus, in Christ's being caused to suffer, we were punished for the wrongs we inflicted on God by our injustice. It is in that way that God's justice is manifested—not God's justice in general, be it noted, but that component of God's justice which is God's retributive justice, the component that consists in God's "inflicting wrath on us" (3:5). And in Christ's becoming just by obeying the requirements of the Torah, we become just. Or, as Paul puts it in the passage before us, God manifests his justice and we become just "through the faithfulness of Jesus Christ" (3:22).[7]

What is it that's required of us in order that Christ be, in the way indicated, our representative? What's required of us for becoming just persons? Or does justification take place entirely over our heads? Only this is required, says Paul: that we believe; that we "receive by faith" (3:25) what Christ has done for our redemption; in short, that we accept Christ as our representative. Christ represents, and thus makes just, those who accept him as their representative. It's not incorrect to speak of "justification by faith"—though all by itself that classically Protestant phrase is an exceedingly lapidary, and potentially misleading, way of putting Paul's point.

Justification has often, perhaps usually, been interpreted as something short of making someone just. It's been understood as declaring someone to be just, or reckoning someone as just, or treating someone as if they were just, and so forth. The hard question that must be put to each such suggestion is: Are persons then in fact just? If declaring someone just is what constitutes God's justification, is the person then in fact just? If reckoning someone as just is what constitutes God's justification, is the person then in fact just? I have interpreted justification as becoming just. Clearly, that's what Paul means when he says that one way to become just is to obey the law; I see no reason to hold that, after saying this, he then, when talking about the new way of becoming just, changed the sense of the word without indicating to his readers that he had done so. Add to this the fact that justification "apart from the law" is understood not as superseding God's justice but as a new, gracious manifestation thereof, and I think it becomes decisively clear that justification consists in becoming a just person—that is, in becoming a person who has not wronged anyone.[8]

## MORE COMMENTS ON TRANSLATING PAUL

I promised a brief comment about how some of the other current English translations handle the issue of translation that I have been wrestling with. But before I get to that, I should take account of an objection that some readers may well raise to my discussion. What entitles me to any views whatsoever as to the proper translation of Paul's *dikai-* stem words in the absence of expertise in Hellenistic Greek, Pharisaic Judaism, the Qumran literature, and the like? I am in no position to do anything other than trust the translators!

My response is that the translators, all of whom I presume to have all the requisite expertise, cannot agree on the translation. Not only are there disagreements among the versions; the versions are internally inconsistent. Some translations think a particular occurrence of the *dikai-* stem is best translated with some grammatical variant of our word "right"; others think it's best translated with some grammatical variant of our word "just." Evidently the linguistic background doesn't settle the issue. What else is to be done in such a case but to look closely at Paul's thought, think carefully about the meanings and connotations of our English words and their grammatical variants, and make the decision in the light of one's conclusions?

A few comments, then, about translations other than the RSV. Through the third chapter in Romans, the New English Bible almost always translates the *dikai-* stem words with grammatical variants on our word "just." The only exception is that on a few occasions it translates the verb "to justify" as "to right wrong." But then, from the fourth chapter onward, it switches and henceforth almost always translates the *dikai-* stem words with grammatical variants on our "righteous." Through Romans 3:23, the New International Version almost always, though again not invariably, translates the *dikai-* stem words with grammatical variants on our word "righteous." It even undertakes a theologically committed paraphrase of "to justify" as "to declare righteous." Then, for the remainder of chapter 3, it switches and consistently uses grammatical variants on our word "just." But then, from the beginning of chapter 4 and onward, it uses variants on "just" and "righteous" in about equal proportion. The Jerusalem Bible is far and away the most nearly consistent. Invariably it translates with variants on our word "just," until it gets to the passage about "being reckoned to Abraham as *dikaiosunê*"; this phrase it translates with variants on our "righteous."

## CONCLUSION: WRONGING GOD
## AND WRONGING OTHERS

It would be appropriate to feel a certain dissatisfaction with my discussion. The question I set out to answer has been answered. The connection between justice and justification is as intimate as it could possibly be. But that's true in a surprising and somewhat discomfiting way. Paul's focus is all on the injustices we have wreaked on God rather than on the injustices we have wreaked on one another. The wrongs done to human beings by human beings seem nowhere in view. Paul's supposedly "God-intoxicated consciousness" seems to have obliterated awareness of all but God and Jesus Christ. Yet, when I initially posed my question "What do justice and justification have to do with each other?" every reader would have understood the justice I was talking about as at least including, if not exhausted by, justice in social relations among human beings.

The major part of the right response to this dissatisfaction is surely that when we look inside the Torah of the Jews and inside the natural law of the Gentiles, what we perceive is that these pertain mostly to justice among human beings. Not entirely; they speak also of our worship of God. But mostly it is justice among human beings that is in view. We've been following Paul in probing the implications of the fact that in treating one's fellow human beings justly, one treats God justly; in wronging one's fellow human beings, one wrongs God. Social justice has an inescapably transcendent dimension; it's on that transcendent dimension that Paul's teaching on justification focuses. And it's that same transcendent dimension that Calvin takes note of in the passage quoted at the very beginning of this essay. No one, says Calvin, "can be injurious to his brother without wounding God himself."

There's another connection. Though I haven't said anything about it, it was certainly not Paul's view that the Torah and natural law have become irrelevant to the person made just in Christ. Such a person has indeed given up on any attempt to become just by fully obeying the law; she sees that as futile. The law serves her nonetheless, as her guide for life in Christ. The person who is justified in Christ pursues justice out of gratitude.

It cannot be denied, however, that Paul's teaching on justification leaves us with difficult questions as to how to regard and treat *in*justice in human relations. If in Christ my fellow human being is a just person, what am I to make of the fact that, as far as I can see, he has wronged me or someone else? What's the place of moral anger and repentance and forgiveness? Are we to operate with some sort of double vision, regarding our fellows as justified in Christ but nonetheless also as having wronged others? Is such double vision possible? Does it make sense? And how are we to engage the injustices of those who do not accept Christ as their representative and hence do not accept the justification offered them?

I think a sort of double vision is indeed what is required. When we are regarded in the light of Christ, our representative, we are indeed just. But we can also be regarded in our own light, as it were; and then we remain in need of sanctification. This is not unlike the judge saying to the young rake standing before him: "When I look at you, what I see is your father; and immediately what comes to mind is what an upstanding citizen he was. So I declare you innocent of the accusations. Now behave yourself." The rake now has a new and powerful reason for curbing his rakish tendencies: he's innocent of the accusations. But it will take some time before the rakish tendencies are eliminated.

Discussing in detail the nature of that double vision which I am here only hinting at will have to await some other occasion. It is enough for now to have discerned the intricate intertwining of justice and justification.

# Contributors

**John W. de Gruchy** is Robert Selby Taylor Professor of Christian Studies and director of the Graduate School in Humanities at the University of Cape Town, South Africa. He is the author of *Liberating Reformed Theology: A South African Contribution to an Ecumenical Debate* (Grand Rapids: Wm. B. Eerdmans Publishing Co., 1991); *Christianity and Democracy* (Cambridge: Cambridge University Press, 1995); and *Christianity, Art and Transformation: Theological Aesthetics in the Struggle for Justice* (Cambridge: Cambridge University Press, 2001).

**Dawn DeVries** is John Newton Thomas Professor of Theology at Union Theological Seminary and Presbyterian School of Christian Education, Richmond, Virginia. She is the author of *Jesus Christ in the Preaching of Calvin and Schleiermacher*, Columbia Series in Reformed Theology (Louisville, Ky.: Westminster John Knox Press, 1996) and the translator and editor of *Servant of the Word: Selected Sermons of Friedrich Schleiermacher*, Fortress Texts in Modern Theology (Philadelphia: Fortress Press, 1987).

**B. A. Gerrish** is John Nuveen Professor Emeritus at the Divinity School, University of Chicago, Illinois. He is the author of *Tradition and the Modern World:*

*Reformed Theology in the Nineteenth Century* (Chicago: University of Chicago Press, 1978) and *Grace and Gratitude: The Eucharistic Theology of John Calvin* (Minneapolis: Fortress Press; Edinburgh: T. & T. Clark, 1993).

**Peter J. Paris** is Elmer G. Homrighausen Professor of Christian Social Ethics at Princeton Theological Seminary, New Jersey. He is the author of *The Social Teaching of the Black Churches* (Philadelphia: Fortress Press, 1985) and *The Spirituality of African Peoples: The Search for a Common Moral Discourse* (Minneapolis: Fortress Press, 1995).

**Jan Rohls** is professor of Systematic Theology and dean of the Protestant Theological Faculty, Ludwig-Maximilians-Universität, Munich, Germany. He is the author of *Reformed Confessions: Theology from Zurich to Barmen*, trans. John Hoffmeyer, Columbia Series in Reformed Theology (Louisville, Ky.: Westminster John Knox Press, 1998); *Protestantische Theologie der Neuzeit*, 2 vols. (Tübingen: J. C. B. Mohr [Paul Siebeck], 1997); and *Geschichte der Ethik*, 2d ed. (Tübingen: J. C. B. Mohr [Paul Siebeck], 1999).

**Nicholas Wolterstorff** is Noah Porter Professor of Philosophical Theology at the Divinity School, Yale University, New Haven, Connecticut. He is the author of *Until Justice and Peace Embrace* (Grand Rapids: Wm. B. Eerdmans Publishing Co., 1983) and *Divine Discourse* (Cambridge: Cambridge University Press, 1995).

# Notes

### Introduction

1. Peter L. Berger, *The Sacred Canopy: Elements of a Sociological Theory of Religion* (Garden City, N. Y.: Doubleday, 1967), 137, 144.
2. David Willis and Michael Welker, eds., *Toward the Future of Reformed Theology: Tasks, Topics, Traditions* (Grand Rapids: Wm. B. Eerdmans Publishing Co., 1999); published first in German as *Zur Zukunft der Reformierten Theologie: Aufgaben, Themen, Traditionen* (Neukirchen-Vluyn: Neukirchener Verlag, 1998).
3. *The Bulletin of the Institute for Reformed Theology* (Richmond, Va.: Union Theological Seminary and Presbyterian School of Christian Education), which began publication in the fall of 1999, endeavors to keep readers abreast of work in the field through news reports as well as articles and reviews.
4. F. E. Mayer, in *The Religious Bodies of America*, 2d ed. (St. Louis: Concordia Publishing House, 1956), dealt with Presbyterians, Congregationalists, Baptists, and Episcopalians in part 4, "The Reformed Bodies," and noted that "in American Lutheran circles the term has usually been employed in a wider sense to include also the Arminian bodies," among whom he locates the Methodists and the Salvation Army in part 5.
5. See, for example, the collection of recent Reformed statements of faith in Lukas Vischer, ed., *Reformed Witness Today: A Collection of Confessions and Statements of*

*Faith Issued by Reformed Churches* (Bern: Evangelische Arbeitsstelle, Oekumene Schweiz, 1982).

6. John Calvin, *Defensio sanae et orthodoxae doctrinae de servitute et liberatione humani arbitrii adversus calumnias Alberti Pighii Campensis* (1543), in *Calvini opera (Corpus Reformatorum)* 6:250 (my translation and emphasis). This gave me the second epigraph I placed at the beginning of the introduction.

7. I suggested this distinction in a lecture, "Tradition in the Modern World: The Reformed Habit of Mind," reprinted in Willis and Welker, eds., *Toward the Future*, 3–20. What follows here is only a brief summary.

8. Preface to A Brief Statement of Faith, *The Constitution of the Presbyterian Church (U.S.A.)*, part 1: *Book of Confessions* (Louisville, Ky.: Office of the General Assembly, 1999), 265.

9. John Calvin, *Institutes of the Christian Religion* 4.1.12; Library of Christian Classics 20–21, ed. John T. McNeill, trans. Ford Lewis Battles (Philadelphia: Westminster Press, 1960), 2:1026.

10. *The Constitution of the Presbyterian Church (U.S.A.)*, part 2: *The Book of Order* (Louisville, Ky.: Office of the General Assembly, 1999), G–2.0500.

11. *Book of Confessions,* 6.191–92.

12. This, my first epigraph, comes from Calvin's *Reply to Cardinal Sadolet's [Sadoleto's] Letter* (1539), as translated in Henry Beveridge, *Calvin's Tracts and Treatises,* 3 vols. (1844–51; reprint, Grand Rapids: Wm. B. Eerdmans Publishing Co., 1958), 1:64.

13. Friedrich Schleiermacher, *On the Galubenslehre: Two Letters to Dr. Lücke,* trans. James Duke and Francis Fiorenza, American Academy of Religion Texts and Translation Series, no. 3 (Chico, Calif.: Scholars Press, 1981), 64.

14. *Inst.* 1.14.4 (1:164).

15. Quoted in Arthur C. Cochrane, ed., *Reformed Confessions of the Sixteenth Century* (Philadelphia: Westminster Press, 1966), 165.

16. *Inst.* 3.11.1 (1:726). Along with justification or forgiveness, Calvin included repentance or sanctification in "the sum of the gospel" (e.g., *Inst.* 3.3.1 [1:592]).

## Chapter 1: Holy Beauty

1. The introduction to *Culture in Another South Africa,* ed. William Campshreuer and Joost Divendal (London: Zed Books, 1989), 12.

2. Sue Williamson, *Resistance Art in South Africa* (Cape Town: David Philip, 1989), 8.

3. See Hans-Georg Gadamer, *The Relevance of the Beautiful and Other Essays* (Cambridge: Cambridge University Press, 1986).

4. Elaine Scarry, *On Beauty and Being Just* (Princeton, N.J.: Princeton University Press, 1999), 57.

5. Theodor W. Adorno, *Aesthetic Theory* (London: Routledge & Kegan Paul, 1984), 72.

6. Ibid., 75.

7. Quoted by Margaret Drabble, *A Writer's Britain: Landscape in Literature* (London: Thames and Hudson, 1979), 224.

8. See Fyodor Dostoyevsky, *The Brothers Karamazov* (London: William Heinemann, 1968), 103.

9. Karl Barth, *Church Dogmatics,* II/1, *The Doctrine of God* (Edinburgh: T. & T. Clark, 1957), 665.

10. See Walter Brueggemann, *Theology of the Old Testament: Testimony, Dispute, Advocacy* (Minneapolis: Fortress Press, 1997), 429.

11. Ibid., 425. See also Samuel Terrien, *The Elusive Presence: Toward a New Biblical Theology* (New York: Harper & Row, 1978).

12. The translation used here is that of the New Revised English Bible.

13. Following the Septuagint, the Jerusalem Bible has "worship Yahweh in his sacred court," thus referring to the holiness of the Temple itself. The New Revised English Bible translates the verse with reference to the holiness of the priestly vestments, echoing the Levitical requirement that Temple priests wear garments ritually clean and appropriate for the occasion (Num. 9:1–14; Lev. 11:24–28).

14. Brueggemann, *Theology of the Old Testament*, 425.

15. It is noteworthy that a conservative evangelical author such as Francis Schaeffer was very critical of the evangelical tendency to exclude visual art from the life of the church and based much of his argument on the use of art in the Temple. Francis A. Schaeffer, *Art and the Bible* (Downers Grove, Ill.: InterVarsity Fellowship, 1973).

16. Barth, *Church Dogmatics*, II/1, 656.

17. Ibid., 666.

18. Karl Barth, *Church Dogmatics*, III/3, *The Doctrine of Creation* (Edinburgh: T. & T. Clark, 1984), 295f.; Karl Barth, "An die Basler Nachrichten" (1952), in *Offene Briefe*, 1945–68 (Zurich: Theologischer Verlag, 1984).

19. Jaroslav Pelikan, *Human Culture and the Holy: Essays on the True, the Good, and the Beautiful* (London: SCM Press, 1959), 124.

20. Augustine, *Confessions and Enchiridion*, book 4, chap. 13; Library of Christian Classics 7 (London: SCM Press, 1955), 88.

21. Karl Barth, *Church Dogmatics*, III/2 (Edinburgh: T. & T. Clark, 1960), 282ff.

22. Ibid., 283.

23. John Calvin, *Institutes of the Christian Religion* 1.11.2–4, 12; Library of Christian Classics 20–21, ed. John T. McNeill, trans. Ford Lewis Battles (Philadelphia: Westminster Press, 1960), 1:100–105, 112.

24. See examples in Hans-Ruedi Weber, *Immanuel: The Coming of Jesus in Art and the Bible* (Grand Rapids: Wm. B. Eerdmans Publishing Co., 1984), and Takenaka Masao and Ron O'Grady, *The Bible through Asian Eyes* (Auckland, N.Z.: Pace, 1991). It is noteworthy that both Weber (a former student of Karl Barth) and Takenaka, who recognize the importance of the artistic representation of Jesus Christ, stand within the Reformed tradition.

25. Calvin, *Inst.* 2.2.15–16 (1:273–75).

26. Ibid., 1.11.12 (1:112).

27. Sergiusz Michalski, *The Reformation and the Visual Arts: The Protestant Image Question in Western and Eastern Europe* (London: Routledge & Kegan Paul, 1993), 71.

28. Karl Barth, *Church Dogmatics*, III/4 (Edinburgh: T. & T. Clark, 1961), 297f.

29. Sara Maitland, *A Big-Enough God: Artful Theology* (London: A. R. Mowbray & Co., 1995), 142f.

30. P. T. Forsyth, *Religion in Recent Art* (London: Hodder & Stoughton, 1905), 2f.

31. P. T. Forsyth, *The Principle of Authority* (1913; reprint, London: Independent Press, 1952), 105ff.

32. P. T. Forsyth, *Christ on Parnassus* (London: Hodder & Stoughton, 1911), 280.

33. Forsyth, *Religion in Recent Art*, 7.

34. Ibid., 145.

35. Ibid., 84f.

36. Frank Burch Brown, *Religious Aesthetics: A Theological Study of Making and Meaning* (Princeton, N. J.: Princeton University Press, 1989), 147.

37. Ibid., 146.

38. Ibid.

39. Ibid., 136.

40. Ibid.

41. Donald Davie, *A Gathered Church: The Literature of the English Dissenting Interest, 1700–1930* (London: Routledge & Kegan Paul, 1978), 25.

42. Brown, *Religious Aesthetics*, 151ff. Cf. Nicholas Wolterstorff, *Art in Action* (Grand Rapids: Wm. B. Eerdmans Publishing Co., 1980), 78ff.
43. Adorno, *Aesthetic Theory*, 342.
44. Christoph Gestrich, *The Return of Splendor in the World* (Grand Rapids: Wm. B. Eerdmans Publishing Co., 1997), 1.
45. Brown, *Religious Aesthetics*, 136.
46. Cf. Adorno, *Aesthetic Theory*, 321.
47. Ibid., 321.
48. Monroe Beardsley, *Aesthetics: Problems in the Philosophy of Criticism* (Indianapolis: Hackett Publishing Co., 1981), 562f.
49. Elza Miles, *Land and Lives: A Story of Early Black Artists* (Cape Town: Human and Rousseau, 1997), 207.
50. Herbert Marcuse, *The Aesthetic Dimension* (Boston: Beacon Press, 1968), 62.
51. Haynes faults Marcuse for the fact that his notion of "the Beautiful" is too morally neutral, as in his affirmation of Leni Riefenstahl's Nazi films as "compelling and 'beautiful.'" Deborah J. Haynes, *The Vocation of the Artist* (Cambridge: Cambridge University Press, 1997), 65.

## Chapter 2: The Theology and Ethics of Martin Luther King Jr.

1. Gayraud S. Wilmore, *Black and Presbyterian: The Heritage and the Hope* (Philadelphia: Geneva Press, 1983), 25.
2. Ibid., 26.
3. Ibid., 94.
4. Ibid.
5. Ibid., 72.
6. Ibid., 84.
7. Martin Luther King Jr., *Stride toward Freedom: The Montgomery Story* (New York: Harper & Row, 1958), 134–35.
8. "Lift Every Voice and Sing," by James Weldon Johnson and J. Rosamond Johnson. Used by permission of Edward B. Marks Music Company.
9. Martin Luther King Jr., *Strength to Love* (New York: Harper & Row, 1968), 97.
10. Ibid., 121.
11. James M. Washington, ed., *A Testament of Hope: The Essential Writings of Martin Luther King, Jr.* (San Francisco: Harper & Row, 1986), 226.
12. Martin Luther King Jr., *Where Do We Go from Here: Chaos or Community?* (New York: Harper & Row, 1967), 37.
13. See King's sermon "The Most Durable Power," in Washington, ed., *Testament of Hope*, 11.
14. See King's "I Have a Dream" speech, in Washington, ed., *Testament of Hope*, 219.

## Chapter 3: Reformed Theology and Modern Culture

1. John Calvin, in *Calvini opera* (*Corpus Reformatorum*) 24:682.
2. Armand Dubourdieu, cited in Myriam Yardeni, "French Calvinist Political Thought 1534–1715," in Menna Prestwich, ed., *International Calvinism, 1541–1715* (Oxford: Clarendon Press, 1985), 335.

## Chapter 4: The Living God

1. Throughout this essay I use masculine pronouns for the Deity. The reason for this is that my own youthful picture of God was certainly a masculine one, and all the

theologians whom I am discussing so identify God. However, anyone who grasps my argument here will undoubtedly understand that, for me, worrying about gender-inclusive or -exclusive language for God simply nurtures an unsophisticated sense of divine personhood that ought to be criticized, not propagated by theologians.

2. "Der Glaube an den Persönlichen Gott," in *Vorträge und Kleinere Arbeiten 1909–1914*, ed. Hans-Anton Drewes and Hinrich Stoevesandt, *Karl Barth Gesamtausgabe* III/3 (Zurich: Theologischer Verlag, 1993), 501. This essay receives a careful treatment in Bruce L. McCormack, *Karl Barth's Critically Realistic Dialectical Theology* (Oxford: Clarendon Press, 1995), 104–7.

3. "Der Glaube," 514–17.

4. Ibid., 519.

5. Ibid., 543.

6. Ibid., 548.

7. Karl Barth, *Die kirchliche Dogmatik* I/1 (Zurich: Evangelischer Verlag A. G. Zollikon, 1947), 47–305. English translation: *Church Dogmatics* I/1, *The Doctrine of the Word of God*, ed. G. W. Bromiley and T. F. Torrance, trans. G. W. Bromiley (Edinburgh: T. & T. Clark, 1975), 47–292. Hereafter cited by volume and page number as KD and ET (English translation). For a discussion of Barth's understanding of God as subject, see James Brown, *Subject and Object in Modern Theology* (New York: Macmillan, 1955), 140–67.

8. KD II/1: 319–34; ET, II/1: 284-97.

9. KD II/1: 320–21; ET, II/1: 285.

10. KD II/1: 322; ET, II/1: 286–87.

11. John Oman, *Grace and Personality* (Cambridge: Cambridge University Press, 1917; 2d ed., 1919), 1–39. An excellent recent study of Oman's theology is Stephen Bevans, *John Oman and His Doctrine of God* (Cambridge: Cambridge University Press, 1992).

12. Oman, *Grace and Personality*, 40–84.

13. Ibid., 64.

14. Ibid., 65.

15. Ibid., 76–77.

16. Emil Brunner, *Wahrheit als Begegnung: Sechs Vorlesungen über das christliche Wahrheitsverständnis* (Berlin: Furche, 1938), 33, 43. English translation: *The Divine-Human Encounter*, trans. Amandus W. Loos (London: SCM Press, 1944), 31, 40.

17. *Wahrheit als Begegnung*, 49–57; ET, 46–54.

18. Herbert H. Farmer, *Revelation and Religion: Studies in the Theological Interpretation of Religious Types* (London: Nisbet & Co., 1954), 1–41.

19. Ibid., 47.

20. Ibid., 48.

21. Ibid., 50.

22. Ibid., 52.

23. Ibid., 55.

24. Ibid., 58.

25. Ibid., 58–59.

26. Ibid., 60.

27. Ibid., 60–65. For more on Farmer's concept of divine personality, see Christopher H. Partridge, *H. H. Farmer's Theological Interpretation of Religion: Towards a Personalist Theology of Religions*, Toronto Studies in Theology 76 (Lewiston, Queenston, Lampeter: Edwin Mellen Press, 1998), 5–16, 184–96.

28. Farmer, *Revelation and Religion*, 66–81.

29. Oman, *Grace and Personality*, v.

30. See, for example, J. Köstlin, "Calvins *Institutio* nach Form und Inhalt in ihrer geschichtlichen Entwicklung," *Theologische Studien und Kritiken* 41 (1868): 7–62, 410–86; Edward A. Dowey, *The Knowledge of God in Calvin's Theology* (New York: Columbia University Press, 1952); T. H. L. Parker, *Calvin's Doctrine of the Knowledge of God*, 2d ed. (Edinburgh: Oliver & Boyd, 1969); B. A. Gerrish, "Theology within the Limits of Piety Alone: Schleiermacher and Calvin's Notion of God," in *The Old Protestantism and the New: Essays on the Reformation Heritage* (Chicago: University of Chicago Press, 1982), 196–207, 375–83; Philip W. Butin, *Revelation, Redemption and Response: Calvin's Trinitarian Understanding of the Divine-Human Relationship* (New York: Oxford University Press, 1995).

31. *Institutio christianae religionis 1559*, in *Ioannis Calvini Opera Selecta*, ed. Peter Barth, Wilhelm Niesel, and Dora Scheuner, 5 vols. (Munich: Chr. Kaiser Verlag, 1926–52), 3:31–64. Hereafter cited by book, chapter, and paragraph as *Inst.*, with page numbers for the Latin (OS) and English (ET) following in parenthesis. All translations are from the standard English translation, *Institutes of the Christian Religion*, Library of Christian Classics 20–21, ed. John T. McNeill, trans. Ford Lewis Battles, 2 vols. (Philadelphia: Westminster Press, 1960).

32. *Inst.* 1.13.1 (OS, 3: 109; ET, 1: 121).

33. For more on Calvin's concept of accommodation, see B. A. Gerrish, "The Reformation and the Rise of Modern Science," in *The Old Protestantism and the New*, 175–76, 364–65; cf. Ford Lewis Battles, "God Was Accommodating Himself to Human Capacity," *Interpretation* 31 (1977): 19–38; David Wright, "Calvin's Accommodating God," in *Calvinus Sincerioris Religionis Vindex: Calvin as the Protector of Pure Religion*, ed. Wilhelm H. Neuser and Brian G. Armstrong, Sixteenth Century Essays and Studies 36 (Kirksville, Mo.: Sixteenth Century Journal Publications, 1997), 3–19; Eric Kayayan, "Accommodation, incarnation et sacrament dans l'Institution de la religion chrètienne de Jean Calvin: L'utilisation de métaphores et de similitudes," *Revue d'Histoire et de Philosophie Religieuses* 75 (1995): 273–87.

34. Commentary on Hebrews 4:15, in *Ioannis Calvini opera quae supersunt omnia*, ed. W. Baum, E. Cunitz, and E. Reuss, 59 vols. (Brunswick and Berlin: Schwetschke and Son, 1863–1900), 55: 53–55. Further references to Calvin's commentaries will be abbreviated Comm., and their location in the *Calvini opera* (hereafter cited as CO) will be given with the volume number followed by a colon and the column number.

35. *Inst.* 2.16.2 (OS, 3: 483–84; ET, 1: 504–5).

36. *Inst.* 1.2.2, 5.9, 10.2, 12.1, 13.21, 13.29; 3.2.6 (OS, 3: 35, 53, 86, 105, 136–37, 151; 4:15; ET, 1: 41, 61–62, 97–98, 116–17, 146–47, 159; 549).

37. *Inst.* 2.13.4 (OS, 3: 458; ET, 1: 481); cf. Comm. John 1:14 (CO 47: 13–16).

38. See Comm. Isa. 45:15–17 (CO 37: 141–43). For a discussion of Calvin's understanding of the hiddenness of God, see B. A. Gerrish, "'To the Unknown God': Luther and Calvin on the Hiddenness of God," in *The Old Protestantism and the New*, 131–49, 334–45.

39. *Inst.* 1.16.3 (OS, 3: 191; ET, 1: 200–201).

40. *Inst.* 1.17.2, 18.4 (OS, 3: 204–5, 225–27; ET, 1: 212–13, 237).

41. Calvin calls the decree of reprobation "horrible" in *Inst.* 3.23.7 (OS, 4: 401; ET, 2: 955), but the underlying tone throughout *Inst.* 3.21–23, is one of defensiveness on behalf of God's justice and goodness.

42. *Inst.* 3.21.5 (OS, 4: 374; ET, 2: 926).

43. *Inst.* 3.22.1, 3.24.5 (OS, 4: 380, 415–16; ET, 2: 933, 970–71). For a discussion of Calvin's warnings against speculation or inordinate curiosity, see E. P. Meijering, *Calvin wider die Neugierde: Ein Beitrag zum Vergleich zwischen reformatorischem*

*und patristichem Denken*, Bibliotheca Humanistica et Reformatorica 29 (Nieuwkoop: B. De Graaf, 1980), esp. 15–25, 31–69.

44. *Inst.* 3.21.3 (OS, 4: 371–72; ET, 2: 924–25). Cf. *Inst.* 3.23.1: "[I]t is wicked to subject to our determination those deep judgments which swallow up all our powers of mind"; *Inst.* 3.23.2: "[I]t is very wicked merely to investigate the causes of God's will"; *Inst.* 3.23.4: "Monstrous indeed is the madness of men, who desire thus to subject the immeasurable to the puny measure of their own reason!" (OS, 4: 394, 395, 398; ET, 2: 948, 949, 952).

45. *Inst.* 1.13.5 (OS, 3: 115; ET, 1: 127).

46. *Inst.* 1.15.4 (OS, 3: 180; ET, 1: 190).

47. *Inst.* 1.13.5 (OS, 3: 115; ET, 1: 127).

48. *Inst.* 1.13.21 (OS, 3: 136; ET, 1: 146).

49. B. A. Gerrish, *Grace and Gratitude: The Eucharistic Theology of John Calvin* (Minneapolis: Fortress Press, 1993), 22–41.

50. See, for example, the discussion of God's "repentance" in *Inst.* 1.17.13 (OS, 3: 217–18; ET, 1: 227).

51. *Inst.* 1.16.8 (OS, 3: 198–200; ET, 1: 207–8). Calvin argues that God's providence is not "empty," "idle," or "unconscious" but "watchful, effective, active . . . [and] engaged in ceaseless activity" (*Inst.* 1.16.3 [OS, 3: 190; ET, 1: 200]).

52. *Reformed Dogmatics: J. Wollebius, G. Voetius, F. Turretin*, ed. and trans. John W. Beardslee III, Library of Protestant Thought (New York: Oxford University Press, 1965), 38.

53. Ibid., 47.

54. Ibid., 39, 47.

55. Ibid., 39.

56. Ibid., 49.

57. Ibid., 93.

58. Friedrich Schleiermacher, *Über die Religion: Reden an die Gebildeten unter ihren Verächtern*, 4th ed. (Berlin: Georg Reimer, 1831), in *Friedrich Schleiermacher: Kritische Gesamtausgabe*, ed. Hans Joachim Birkner et al. (Berlin: Walter De Gruyter, 1984– ), I/12: 146; hereafter cited by division, volume, and page number as KGA; English translation, *On Religion: Speeches to Its Cultured Despisers*, trans. John Oman (New York: Harper & Row, 1958), 116.

59. For more on Schleiermacher's critique of anthropomorphism, see Franz Christ, *Menschlich von Gott Reden: Das Problem des Anthropomorphismus bei Schleiermacher* (Gütersloh: Gütersloher Verlagshaus Gerd Mohn, 1982), esp. 95–128; cf. Julia A. Lamm, *The Living God: Schleiermacher's Theological Appropriation of Spinoza* (University Park, Pa.: Penn State University Press, 1996).

60. KGA, I/12: 120–21; ET, 95.

61. KGA, I/12: 123; ET, 97.

62. KGA, I/12: 125–26; ET, 99.

63. KGA, I/12: 128; ET, 101. Here Schleiermacher is echoing Plato's argument in the *Laws* that one of three forms of practical atheism is when people believe that if they "pay the gods a trifle in the way of sacrifice and flattery, they will lend their help in vast frauds and deliver the sinner from all sorts of heavy penalties." Plato calls this form of atheism the "creed of the worst, who are the majority" (*Laws* 12.948c).

64. KGA, I/12: 148–49; ET, 118.

65. KGA, I/12: 146; ET, 116.

66. Friedrich Schleiermacher, *Der christliche Glaube nach den Grundsätzen der evangelischen Kirche im Zusammenhange dargestellt*, 7th ed., based on the 2d German ed., ed. Martin Redeker, 2 vols. (Berlin: Walter de Gruyter, 1960), §§ 3–4; English translation, *The Christian Faith*, ed. H. R. Mackintosh and J. S. Stewart

(Edinburgh: T. & T. Clark, 1928; paperback reprint, 1999), 3–18. Hereafter cited by paragraph and section as *Gl.*, with the page number in the English translation following ET.

67. *Gl.*, § 50; ET, 194.
68. *Gl.*, § 50.1; ET, 195.
69. *Gl.*, § 51; ET, 200–203.
70. *Gl.*, § 52; ET, 203.
71. *Gl.*, § 53; ET, 206.
72. *Gl.*, § 54; ET, 211.
73. *Gl.*, § 54.4; ET, 216–18.
74. *Gl.*, § 55; ET, 219.
75. *Gl.*, § 55.1; ET, 221.
76. *Gl.*, § 55.2; ET, 225.
77. *Gl.*, § 55.2; ET, 225–26.
78. *Gl.*, § 83; ET, 341.
79. *Gl.*, § 84; ET, 345.
80. *Gl.*, § 83.3; ET, 344.
81. *Gl.*, § 85; ET, 353–54.
82. *Gl.*, § 167.1; ET, 730.
83. *Gl.*, § 167.2; ET, 731.
84. *Gl.*, § 166; ET, 727.
85. *Gl.*, § 168; ET, 732.
86. *Gl.*, § 169; ET, 735.
87. *Gl.*, §§ 168.1, 169; ET, 733, 735–37.
88. A. Emanuel Biedermann, "Über die Persönlichkeit Gottes: Mit besonderer Berücksichtigung von Strauss' Glaubenslehre und Rosenkranz' Recension derselben," *Tübinger theologische Jahrbücher* (1842): 205–87.
89. *God and Incarnation in Mid-Nineteenth Century German Theology: G. Thomasius, I. A. Dorner, A. E. Biedermann*, ed. and trans. Claude Welch, Library of Protestant Thought (New York: Oxford University Press, 1965), 307–10. Biedermann developed his own psychology of knowledge. All knowledge begins with perception (*Wahrnehmen*); when we present our percepts to ourselves as objects for reflection, they become representations (*Vorstellungen*); finally, when we purify our representations of the inevitable sensuous attachments to them, we have rational thought (*Denken*). Biedermann believed all knowledge arose in this way, and that it had to follow the order from perception to representation to pure thought. See the editor's discussion in *God and Incarnation*, 16, 20, 289n.4.
90. Ibid., 361.
91. Ibid., 364.
92. Jürgen Moltmann, *The Crucified God: The Cross of Christ as the Foundation and Criticism of Christian Theology* (New York: Harper & Row, 1974); William C. Placher, *Narratives of a Vulnerable God: Christ, Theology, and Scripture* (Louisville, Ky.: Westminster John Knox, 1994). Alfred North Whitehead proposes that God, in his consequent nature, is "our great companion—the fellow-sufferer who understands" (*Process and Reality: An Essay in Cosmology* [New York: Macmillan Co., 1929; reprint, New York: Humanities Press, 1955], 532). I regret that within the limits of the present essay I have not been able to consider the process theologians' arguments for divine personality. However, it is important to bear in mind that the process theologians, including Whitehead and Charles Hartshorne, recognize the symbolic character of God-language and thus by no means argue for a simplistic understanding of divine personhood. See Whitehead, *Process and Reality*, 525; cf. Charles Hartshorne, *Man's Vision of God and the Logic of Theism* (Chicago and New

York: Willet Clark, 1941), 249–50; idem, *The Divine Relativity: A Social Conception of God* (New Haven, Conn.: Yale University Press, 1948), xi–xii, 142–47; Charles Hartshorne and William L. Reese, *Philosophers Speak of God* (Chicago and London: University of Chicago Press, 1953), 22–23.

93. A recent poll of the membership of the elite National Academy of Sciences showed that only 7 percent of its members believed in a "personal God" who would listen to their prayers (cited in Natalie Angier, "Confessions of a Lonely Atheist," *New York Times Magazine*, January 14, 2001, 37). See the discussion of scientific faith in B. A. Gerrish, *Saving and Secular Faith: An Invitation to Systematic Theology* (Minneapolis: Fortress Press, 1999), 43, 80–81.

94. The Westminster Confession (1647), chapter 2, in *Die Bekenntnisschriften der reformierten Kirche, in authentischen Texten mit geschichtlicher Einleitung und Register,* ed. E. F. Karl Müller (Leipzig: A. Deichert [Georg Böhme], 1903), 547–48.

95. The subject of divine personality continued to be a focus of theological interest in the twentieth century. See, for example, J. M. E. McTaggart, *Some Dogmas of Religion* (London: Edward Arnold, 1906), 186–220; Ian T. Ramsey, "A Personal God," in *Prospect for Theology: Essays in Honor of H. H. Farmer* (Digswell Place, Welwyn: James Nisbet, 1966), 53–71; *A Personal God?* ed. Edward Schillebeeckx and Bas van Iersel, *Concilium* 103 (New York: Seabury, 1977). See also *Persons, Divine and Human,* ed. Christoph Schwöbel and Colin E. Gunton (Edinburgh: T. & T. Clark, 1991). This book actually focuses more on the theological anthropology that can be developed in connection with a renewed appreciation for the social doctrine of the Trinity. Also pertinent are Vincent Brümmer, *Speaking of a Personal God: An Essay in Philosophical Theology* (Cambridge: Cambridge University Press, 1992); Gerald Bray, *The Personal God: Is the Classical Understanding of God Tenable* (Carlisle: Paternoster Press, 1998). Bray attempts a response to the "open theism" of evangelical theologian Clark Pinnock and others.

## Chapter 5: Justice and Justification

1. Let me call attention to one exception, Kathryn Tanner's article, "Justification and Justice in a Theology of Grace," in *Theology Today* 55(1999), 510-23. To my regret, I have not been able to engage Tanner's article here; so let me just say that though I probe some points that she passes over rather quickly, and she, some that I pass over quickly, there is nonetheless a great deal of convergence between our treatments—along, admittedly, with some disagreement here and there.

2. The only difference between the RSV and the NRSV, on the points I will be raising, occurs in the translation of Romans 5: 21. The RSV translates the passage this way: "so that, as sin reigned in death, grace also might reign through righteousness." The NRSV translates it as follows: "so that, just as sin exercised dominion in death, so grace might also exercise dominion through justification." A footnote is attached to "justification" saying, "Or *righteousness.*" I interpret this footnote as meaning that the translators do not wish us to read any particular significance into the change in their translation from "righteousness" in the RSV to "justification" in the NRSV. Yet, if that is how the footnote is to be understood, I am at a loss to understand why they bothered to make the change. The Greek has *dia dikaiosunê.* If my scrutiny has been correct, every other occurrence of *dikaiosunê* in Romans is translated by the RSV (and the NRSV) as "righteousness." Why, then, in this revision of the RSV, the translators made this change, I do not understand. Even more mysterious is why, if they wanted to move away from "righteousness," they would translate the phrase as "through justification" when the Greek has, literally, "through justice."

3. J. Louis Martyn, *Galatians: A New Translation with Introduction and Commentary* (New York: Doubleday, 1997). Page numbers to this commentary are hereafter cited in the text.

4. Perhaps one can wrong other beings than persons; if so, then I should speak of someone *or something* being wronged.

5. This is also clear from 3:20, where Paul says that "no human being will be justified in God's sight by works of the law." (RSV). The suggestion is clearly that if anyone did fully obey the law, they would thereby be justified. And what "justified" had to mean here is, clearly, *become just*.

6. With the exception that Romans 4:7–8 is a quotation of the opening lines of Psalm 32, in which the psalm writer says, "Happy are those whose transgression is forgiven, whose sin is covered."

7. The Greek is *dia pisteôs Jesou Christou*. The RSV translates this "through faith in Jesus Christ" for all who believe. This seems to me indubitably a mistranslation. "Jesus Christ" is in the genitive in the Greek. Paul is not speaking of *our* faith *in* Christ but of the faith *of* Christ—that is, *Christ's* faith. It's hard to see what could be behind this mistranslation other than the reading into Paul's text, once again, of a certain strand of Protestant theology. On the proper translation of the phrase, see Martyn's *Galatians*, 270–71.

8. The interpretation I have come to is thus a version of the traditional "imputation" view.

# Index of Scriptural Citations

## Old Testament

**Genesis**
3:1–19          37

**Leviticus**
11:24–28        101 n.13

**Numbers**
9:1–14          101 n.13

**Deuteronomy**
10:18           83
23:19–21        48

**Psalms**
32:1            108 n.6
96:9            17

**Isaiah**
6:1–13          16–17
45:15           71

## New Testament

**Matthew**
5:6             84
5:10            84
18:22           35

**Luke**
6:34            48

**John**
1:14            20
3:16            30

**Romans**
1:17            93
2:13–14         92
2:14–15         91
3:5             85, 92, 94
3:19            91
3:20            92, 108 n.5
3:21–26         84–85, 92–94
4:1–12          86
4:7–8           108 n.7
4:22–25         86
5:1             91
5:10–11         91
12:1–2          18

**1 Corinthians**
3:16            17
6:19            17
13:13           35

**Galatians**
4:19            21

**1 John**
1:1             16
4:16            78

# Index of Persons

Abraham, 86, 95
Adorno, Theodor, 14, 23, 24
Ailly, Pierre d', 52
Allen, Richard, 34
Althusius, John, 51
Amyraut, Moise, 52, 53
Aristotle, 56
Arminius, Jacobus, 59
Augustine, 18, 58, 64, 72

Balthasar, Hans Urs von, 15
Barnett, Ida Wells, 34
Barth, Karl, 4, 10, 15, 18, 19, 20, 21, 59, 67,
    69, 80
  on God as person, 62–64
Bayle, Pierre, 52
Beardsley, Monroe, 24
Bekker, Balthasar, 57
Berger, Peter, 2, 99 n.1
Beza, Theodore, 48, 50, 51, 52, 58, 59

Biedermann, A[lois] E., 10, 62, 63, 79–80
Bradley, F[rancis] H., 69
Bretschneider, Karl Gottlieb, 59
Brown, Frank Burch, 22–23, 24
Brueggemann, Walter, 17
Brunner, [Heinrich] Emil, 10, 62, 66, 69, 70,
    80
Buber, Martin, 63, 66
Bucer, Martin, 50
Bullinger, Heinrich, 58
Burroughs, Nannie, 34

Calvin, John, 1, 4, 5, 6, 9, 10, 19, 20, 23, 47,
    48, 49, 50, 55, 57, 62, 74, 76, 77, 83,
    96
  on art, 53–54
  on church government, 50
  on civil government, 51–52
  on election, 58–59, 71–72
  on God, 70–73

Calvin *(continued)*
  on science, 56
  on usury, 47–48
Clauberg, Johannes, 56
Cocceius, Johannes, 58
Copernicus, Nicolaus, 56
Cornish, Samuel, 28
Cozart, Leland Stanford, 9, 28

Danaeus, Lambertus, 56, 57
Daniel, 39
Davie, Donald, 23
Descartes, René, 56
Dostoyevsky, Fyodor, 15
Du Bois, Jacob, 56
Dubourdieu, Armand, 53
Duplessis-Mornay, Philippe, 50, 51, 52

Edwards, Jonathan, 4, 15
Elaw, Zilpha, 34
Erastus, Thomas, 50

Farmer, H[erbert] H., 10, 62, 66–69, 70, 80
Fichte, Johann Gottlieb, 63
Forsyth, P[eter] T., 21

Galilei, Galileo, 57
Gandhi, Mahatma, 30
Garnett, Henry Highland, 28
Gestrich, Christoph, 23
Gordimer, Nadine, 13
Grimke, Francis, 28
Grünewald, Matthias, 20

Hartshorne, Charles, 106 n.92
Haynes, Deborah J., 102 n.51
Hegel, G[eorg] W. F., 53, 79, 80
Henry IV, Henry of Navarre, 52
Herrmann, Wilhelm, 63
Hobbes, Thomas, 89
Hodge, Charles, 5
Hôpital, Michel de l', 52
Hotman, François, 50, 51
Hundeshagen, Karl Bernhard, 58
Hurault, Michel, 52

Isaiah, 16, 18, 22, 71

Jesus, 27–28, 30, 32, 34, 35, 37, 38, 42, 63, 71, 93
  ethnic particularity of, 27–28
  teaching of, 30, 35, 38, 65
John the Baptist, 20

John of Damascus, 77
John Sigismund, Elector of Brandenburg, 59
Johnson, James Weldon, 33
Jonah, 39
Jung, Carl Gustav, 69
Jurieu, Pierre, 53

Kant, Immanuel, 76
King, Martin Luther, Jr., 9, chap. 2 passim
  his vocation as prophet, 31, 32
Kuyper, Abraham, 9, 10, 46, 50, 53, 54, 55, 57

Lawrence, D[avid] H., 15, 23
Lee, Jarena, 34
Leydecker, Melchior, 37
Louis XIV, 53
Luther, Martin, 5, 10, 11, 47, 57

MacIntyre, Alisdair, 89
Maitland, Sara, 21
Marcuse, Herbert, 25
Marsilius of Padua, 52
Martyn, Louis, 85, 93
Marvell, Andrew, 20
Marx, Karl, 36
Mayer, F. E., 99 n.4
Miles, Elsa, 24
Milton, John, 20
Moltmann, Jürgen, 40, 50
Monsell, John, 17
Moses, 37, 48, 56, 83
Mozart, Wolfgang Amadeus, 20

Occam (Ockham), William, 52
Olevian, Caspar, 58
Oman, John, 10, 62, 64–66, 69, 70
Otto, Rudolf, 69

Pasolini, Pier Paolo, 20
Paul, 11, 70
  on justice and justification, chap. 5 passim
Pelagius, 64
Pennington, J. W. C., 28
Peter of Mastricht, 57
Pighius, Albert, 1, 5
Plato, 105 n.63

Rembrandt, Harmensz, van Rijn, 55
Rubens, Peter Paul, 54

Sadoleto, Jacopo, 1, 7
Scarry, Elaine, 14
Schaeffer, Francis A., 101 n.15

Schleiermacher, Friedrich, 4, 5, 10, 58, 61, 62,
    64, 67, 80
    on divine personality, 74–79
Schneckenburger, Matthias, 58
Schweizer, Alexander, 57, 58, 59
Sidney, Philip, 20
Spenser, Edmund, 20
Spinoza, Baruch, 63, 74
Strauss, David Friedrich, 79

Takenaka Masao, 101 n.24
Tanner, Kathryn, 107 n.1
Terrell, Mary Church, 34
Tillich, Paul, 10, 40, 42, 69
Troeltsch, Ernst, 9, 10, 45–46, 49–50, 57
Truth, Sojourner, 34
Tubman, Harriet, 34

Van Dyck, Anthony, 54
Voetius, Gisbert, 56, 57, 59

Weber, Hans-Ruedi, 101 n.24
Weber, Max, 9, 10, 45–46, 47, 57
Whitehead, Alfred North, 106 n.92
Wieman, Henry Nelson, 68
William of Orange, 53
Wilmore, Gayraud S., 5, 9, 27–28, 29, 42, 43
Wittich, Christoph, 56
Wollebius, Johannes, 73–74, 76
Wright, Theodore S., 28

Zanchi, Girolamo, 56, 57
Zwingli, Ulrich, 50, 54

# Index of Subjects

absolutism, 52, 53
accommodation, 10, 20, 56, 57, 70–71, 74
activity, moral, 42, 47, 58
aestheticism, 15, 18, 53
aesthetics, 8–9, chap. 1 passim
  meaning of, 14
  Reformed perspective on, 16
African Americans, 9, chap. 2 passim, 90
  "national anthem" of, 33
  spiritual, 91
Amboise, conspiracy of, 51
analogy, 18, 22, 73, 77, 79, 80, 81, 91
anthropomorphism, 62, 74–75, 77, 78, 80, 81
apartheid, 8, 13, 14, 23, 30
architecture, 23
Arminianism, 6, 48, 55, 64
art, 8–9, chap. 1 passim, 53–55
  as antiestablishment, 24
  black, 24
  atheism, 75

atonement, 6
  *See also* Christ
autonomy, 65

Beatitudes, 66
beauty, chap. 1 passim
  and aesthetics, 14
  of God, 15, 17, 18, 21
  and goodness, 15, 23
  and holiness, 16–19, 22, 25
  saving, 20
begging, 49
Bible, 4, 5, 7, 11, 16, 34, 35, 37, 40, 41, 48, 55, 56, 57, 61, 66, 67, 69, 71, 73, 74, 80
  inerrancy of, 6
  mysteries of, 72
  translations of, chap. 5 passim
Black Church movement, 34
*Book of Concord*, 1
*Book of Confessions*, 4

Calvinism, 1, 2, 8, 9–10, 23, 45, 46
    central dogma of, 57, 58
    ethic of, 45
    five points of, 6
    and modern culture, chap. 3 passim
    neo-, 16
capitalism, 9, 10, 45, 47–49, 50
Catholicism, Roman, 1, 2, 5, 45–46, 49, 54,
    57
causality, 77, 78, 79
censures, church, 49, 50
character, moral, 88
charity, 48, 90
Christ, 6, 18, 21, 27, 29, 30, 61, 63, 85, 96
    crucified, 20, 21, 25, 32, 35, 86, 91
    divinity of, 67
    images of, 19, 20
    incarnation of, 20, 25, 27, 30, 32, 38, 67,
        74
    as Lamb of God, 30
    as liberator, 28
    as mediator, 71
    miracles of, 6
    as mirror of election, 72
    monarchy of, 50
    as Redeemer, 40, 93
    as representative, 85, 94, 96
    resurrection of, 6, 25, 28, 32, 86
    as Savior, 71
    second coming of, 6
    as Son, 68, 71, 91
    virgin birth of, 6, 71
    work of, 6, 84
    See also Jesus
churches, Reformed, 3, 4
    World Alliance of (WARC), 3
    See also Presbyterians
Commandments, the Ten, 17
    Second Commandment, 18, 54
    Eighth Commandment, 48
commands, 91
community, 39, 41, 42
    the beloved, 9, 35, 36, 41
confessions, 1, 3, 7, 57, 59
    Brief Statement of Faith, 5
    Heidelberg Catechism, 59
    Scots, 8
    subscription to, 4
    Westminster, 4, 81
conscience, 21, 22, 35, 42, 78
consistory, 50, 51
contract, political, 51, 52
cooperation with God, 38, 39

correlation, 40, 41
Counter-Reformation, 49, 53
covenant, 6, 7, 31, 58
creation, 18, 37, 38, 39, 41, 48, 55, 56, 73, 76,
    77
    as moral order, 78
    the new, 30
creativity, 14, 15, 16, 19, 20, 21, 24, 65, 68
cross, crucifixion, 21, 35, 38, 71
culture, modern, 10, chap. 3 passim
curiosity, 7, 72

decree(s), God's eternal, 58, 71, 73–74
democracy, 9, 13, 46, 49–53, 57
dependence, 65, 66
    absolute, 58, 67, 76, 78, 79
desire, 39
disobedience, civil
    See resistance
dispensationalism, 6
distinctives, Reformed, 6–5, 11
doctrine, 1, 5, 6, 8–10, 79, 83
    as expression of piety, 76–77
dogma
    See doctrine
dogmatics, 76–77, 79
Dort, Synod of, 6, 48, 58, 59
drama, 53
duty, 88, 89, 90, 91

economics, 9
election
    See predestination
election of ministers and elders, 51
Enlightenment, 59, 89
equality, 29, 34, 35, 57
eternity, 76, 77
ethics, 11, 13, 16, 22, 30–36, 39, 40, 43, 48,
    49, 54, 83, 88
Eucharist, 10, 68, 71
Euro-Americans, 29, 32
evil, evils, 36, 37, 38, 39, 41, 78, 81, 90
exodus, 31, 38
experience, 63, 64, 65, 69, 71, 72, 76, 80, 93
expiation, 85

faith, 16, 21, 22, 32, 33, 34, 37, 39, 40, 41, 44,
    48, 66, 67, 70, 78, 79, 81, 85, 93, 94
    crisis of, 62
    fruits of, 47
    reckoned as righteousness, 86
    and works, 58
faithfulness of Jesus Christ, 94, 108 n.7

forgiveness, 35, 38, 93–94
Formula Helvetica, 58
freedom, 32, 33, 34, 35, 36, 38, 41, 65, 77,
    of God, 64
    relative, 76
    *See also* will, free
fundamentalism, 6

Gentiles, 92, 96
God, 6, 37
    absence of, 61
    as the absolute, 64
    anger of, 11, 71, 85, 91, 92, 94, 96
    as arbitrary, 65, 72
    as artist, 77, 78
    attributes of, 70, 71, 73, 74, 76, 77, 78,
        79, 86
    beauty of, 15, 18, 21
    as creator, 16, 17, 20, 32, 37, 40, 55, 70
    design of, 35, 37
    and ethics, 30–36
    as the Exalted, 63, 80
    as Father (parent), 34, 36, 65, 68, 72
    as fountain of good, 72
    as friend, 9, 34, 37, 38
    glory of, 7, 17, 19, 58, 85
    goodness of, 37
    as helper, 36, 75
    hiddenness of, 10, 62, 71–73
    infinity of, 73
    as irresistible force, 64
    as judge, 40
    as just, 30, 31
    knowledge of, 7, 63, 69, 70, 71, 72, 76
    as liberator and redeemer, 9, 31–36, 70
    living, 75
    love of, 30, 35, 61, 63, 64, 65, 68, 76, 78
    majesty of, 19, 20
    mercy of, 6
    mystery of, 20
    normative concept of, 69
    otherness of, 67, 73, 74
    as person, 10, 32, chap. 4 passim
    philosophical concept of, 66
    and political contracts, 51
    power of, 21, 38, 41, 68
    pronouns for, 102–3 n.1
    simplicity of, 73–74
    as source of goodness, being, and value, 36,
        67
    sovereignty of, 6, 9, 10, 31, 32, 35, 36, 39,
        42, 50, 57
    spirituality of, 79

as subject, 63
    symbols for, 69
    trustworthiness of, 38–39
    as "whence," 76
    will of, 47, 51, 65, 71, 72, 77
    wisdom of, 61, 76, 78
goodness, 15, 32, 36, 37, 78, 88
gospel, 6, 7, 8, 10, 19, 22, 29, 30, 34, 39, 71, 93
grace, 6, 20, 32, 41, 42, 54, 57, 64, 65, 69, 76,
        85, 93
    common (universal), 55, 59
    free, 58
gratitude, 96
guilt, 88, 89, 90, 91, 93

habits of mind, 5–6, 7–8
hatred, 41
heaven, 6, 71
hell, 6
Hellenism, 19, 21
holiness, 17, 18, 22, 48, 76, 78
hope, 31, 32, 33, 35, 37, 39, 40
Huguenots, 23, 52, 53
humanism, 7, 38
humanity, 9, 19, 28, 29, 32, 33, 34, 35, 36,
        38, 66, 70
hymns, 76
    "Lift Every Voice," 33
    "Worship the Lord," 17

iconoclasm, 15, 18, 23
icons, 20, 25
idolatry, 8, 10, 19, 22, 23, 70, 81
image of God (*imago dei*), 23, 28, 32, 38, 52, 83
images, 19, 20, 21, 22, 23, 25, 79, 80
imagination, 14, 15, 16, 17, 19, 21, 22, 25
immortality, 75
imputation, 108 n.8
incarnation, 20, 27, 32, 37, 67, 71, 74
Independents, 52
individualism, 87
individuality, 63
infralapsarianism, 58
injury, moral, 89
    *See also* wrongs
injustice, 13, 18, 25, 34, 90, 96
integration, 42
I-Thou relationship, 63, 66, 68–69, 80, 81

Judaism, 11, 83, 92, 95, 96
justice, 6, 8, 13, 14, 15, 16, 17, 18, 21, 24, 30,
        31, 32, 34, 38, 39, 40–41, 42, 51, 76,
        78, chap. 5 passim

justice *(continued)*
  economic, 23
  racial, 29, 30, 42
  reckoned, 86
  and righteousness, 11, 90
  social, 34, 96
justification, 10–11, 57, 58, chap. 5 passim
  as becoming just, 94

kingdom of God, 27, 35, 42, 84

law, 42, 85, 92, 93, 94
  natural, 92, 96
liberalism, 46, 48, 49, 53
  Protestant, 62–63
liberation, 13, 28, 30, 38
liberty
  *See* freedom
literature, 21, 35
love, 9, 30, 31, 32, 35, 38, 39, 40–42, 64, 66, 68, 76, 78, 88
Lutheranism, 1, 2, 4, 7, 9, 10, 11, 45, 46, 50, 52, 54, 57, 58, 59, 63, 71

mercy, 6, 18, 31, 78, 90, 93
metaphor, 15, 17, 72, 75, 78, 80, 89
militarism, 30
miracle, 6, 62
modernity, 46, 55
monarchomachists, 50, 51, 52
monarchy, 52, 53
moral condition, 92
moral relationship to God, 92
moral theory
  *See* ethics
music, 9, 33, 53, 55, 88

Nantes, Edict of, 52, 53
nature, 55, 57, 71, 77, 79
  laws of, 73, 77, 81
  as theater, 23, 56, 78
necessity, 77
Neoplatonism, 64
neo-Stoicism, 49, 54
neo-Thomism, 46

obligation
  *See* duty
omnipotence, 76, 77
omnipresence, 76, 77
omniscience, 76, 77, 78
oppression, 28, 30, 34, 41
order, moral, 78, 89

orthodoxy, 75
  Eastern, 3
  Reformed, 56, 57, 58, 62, 73

painting, 9, 20, 53–55
pantheism, 74
personality, concept of, 61, 63
philistinism, 23
philosophy, 15, 35, 63, 66, 72
  Christian, 7
  *See* ethics
pietism, 2
piety, 8, 10, 18, 59, 61, 67, 68, 74, 75, 80, 81
  "teleological," 58
pluralism, 2–3
politics, 9
Politiques, 52
poverty, 23, 30, 34, 48
power, 40–42
  black, 40
  God's, 21, 38, 41, 68
  spiritual ("soul force"), 41, 42
praxis, 42
prayer, 33, 61–62, 67, 80
  Lord's, 66
predestination, 6, 10, 45, 47, 48, 49, 54, 55, 57, 58, 59, 71–72, 73
Presbyterians, 3, 4, 9, 27, 28, 29, 42, 43
  old school, 6
promise, 32
promised land, 31
prophets, 34, 38, 85
Protestantism, 45, 46, 47, 57, 85
  old and new, 59
  *See also* Lutheranism
providence, 20, 36–38, 47, 65, 71
Puritans, 20, 23, 47

Qumran, 11, 95

racism, chap. 2 passim
rationalism, 2, 64
reason, 32, 76
reciprocity (of God and creation), 76, 77, 78
reconciliation, 41, 91, 93
redemption, 18, 21, 25, 28, 30, 32, 39, 41, 76, 78, 85, 91, 93, 94
Reformation, the Protestant, 1, 5, 6, 7, 8, 10, 38, 47, 48, 51, 66
regeneration, 21
religion, concept of, 58–59, 66–67
Renaissance, the, 7, 38

repentance, 96
representation, 79–80
reprobation, 59
*Rerum novarum*, 46
resistance, 33, 39, 50, 51, 52
    nonviolent, 9, 30, 31, 35, 36, 41
revelation, 10, 19, 21, 63, 64, 66, 67, 69, 70,
    71, 72, 78, 80
revolution
    English, 52, 53
    French, 46
    Industrial, 46
righteousness
    *See* justice
rights
    civil, 41
    God's, 91, 92
    moral, 89, 90
    natural, 89
Romanticism, 14, 18, 64

sacraments, 71
salvation, 6, 15, 40, 59, 71
sanctification, 7, 16, 22–25, 49, 58, 96
Saumur, Academy of, 52
scholasticism, Protestant, 73–74
science, natural, 9, 10, 53, 55–57, 81
science, social, 15, 35
sculpture, 20, 53
Sedan, Academy of, 52
segregation, 32, 33
Sermon on the Mount, 30, 35
sin, 22, 23, 55, 71, 76, 78, 85, 86, 92, 93
slavery, 28, 29, 32, 33, 34, 37, 39
sovereignty
    of God, 6, 9, 10, 31, 32, 35, 36, 39, 42,
        50, 57
    of the king, 52
    of the people, 50, 52
speculation, 7, 72
Spinozism, 59
    *See also* Spinoza
Spirit, 9, 19, 20, 21, 22, 25, 32, 56, 68, 80
    absolute, 79
    "being spirit," 63
    and human creativity, 16
    infinite, 79, 80
Stoicism, 64
subjectivity, 87
suffering, 28, 31, 33, 34, 36, 37, 39, 41, 61,
    71, 75
    Christ's, 20, 39, 94
*summum bonum*, 41

supralapsarianism, 58
syllogism, practical, 48
symbol, 15, 17, 19, 69

taste, 22–25
Temple, the, 17, 18
tenets, essential, 5, 6, 7–8
theodicy, 36–38
theology
    confessional, 2–3
    dialectical, 66
    dogmatic, 79, 80
    evangelical, 2, 5, 8, 10, 17
    mediating, 63
    natural, 66
    neo-orthodox, 66
    practical, 7, 70
    process, 106 n.92
    Protestant, 85, 87, 94, 108 n.7
    Reformed, 3–8, 9, 11, chap. 3 passim
time, 77
tolerance, 52, 53
Torah, 92, 94, 96
tradition, 2, 3, 4–5, 7, 22, 85
    African American, 30, 31, 34, 36, 37, 42,
        43
    Black Christian, 28, 29, 40
    free church, 32
    racist, 32
    Reformed, 3, 4, 5–6, 15, 17, 30, 62, 70,
        80
transformation, 21, 22–25, 29
    personal, 7, 17
    social, 7, 8, 9, 13, 16, 22–25, 40, 43
    *See also* ethics, sanctification
Trent, Council of, 1
Trinity, 16, 67, 70, 72

ugliness, chap. 1 passim
usury, 47–48

Vatican Council, the First, 46
victory over evil, 36–37, 38
vocation
    Luther on, 47
    Martin Luther King's, 31–32
    theological, 62

war, impact on theology, 69
Wars of Religion, 52
will, free, 36, 48, 59, 64
Word, 20, 28, 66, 71, 72, 73
works, 58, 92

world
  as good, 78
  as theater of redemption, 78
  *See also* creation, nature
worship, 7, 17, 18, 22, 31, 32, 33, 34, 55, 67,
  68, 80, 88, 96

wrath
  *See* God, anger of
wrongs, 89, 90, 91, 92, 93, 94, 96

# Reformed Theology for the
# Third Christian Millennium

.